The Splendour Falls

MERCER
UNIVERSITY PRESS

Endowed by
TOM WATSON BROWN
and
THE WATSON-BROWN FOUNDATION, INC.

The Splendour Falls

Essays

Sam Pickering

MERCER UNIVERSITY PRESS
MACON, GEORGIA

MUP/ P470

© 2013 Mercer University Press
1400 Coleman Avenue
Macon, Georgia 31207
All rights reserved

First Edition

Books published by Mercer University Press are printed on acid-free paper that meets the requirements of the American National Standard for Information Sciences—Permanence of Paper for Printed Library Materials.

Mercer University Press is a member of Green Press Initiative (greenpressinitiative.org), a nonprofit organization working to help publishers and printers increase their use of recycled paper and decrease their use of fiber derived from endangered forests. This book is printed on recycled paper.

Library of Congress Cataloging-in-Publication Data
Pickering, Samuel F., 1941-
  The splendour falls : essays / Sam Pickering. -- First edition.
     pages cm
  ISBN-13: 978-0-88146-449-8 (pbk. : alk. paper)
  ISBN-10: 0-88146-449-X (pbk. : alk. paper)
 1. Pickering, Samuel F., 1941---Travel. 2. American essays. I. Title.
  AC8.P6728 2013
  081--dc23
                          2013027502

Contents

Introduction	1
In the Evening	10
Voices	21
The Purposeless Life	34
Time Out	47
Walking	58
Goings	77
Brabblement	86
Shopping	98
Tarry	105
The Last Exam	115
Birthday	123
When Found	130
Calm	139
My Secret Life	149
Not all Three	158
Committed	164
Morning Sickness	174
Tourist at Home	184
Afterword	193

Books by Sam Pickering

Essay Collections
A Continuing Education
The Right Distance
May Days
Still Life
Let It Ride
Trespassing
The Blue Caterpillar
Living to Prowl
Deprived of Unhappiness
A Little Fling
The Last Book
The Best of Pickering
Indian Summer
Autumn Spring
Journeys
Dreamtime

Travel
Walkabout Year
Waltzing the Magpies
Edinburgh Days
A Tramp's Wallet

Literary Studies
The Moral Tradition in English Fiction, 1785-1850
John Locke and Children's Books in Eighteenth-Century England
Moral Instruction and Fiction for Children, 1749-1820

Teaching
Letters to a Teacher

Memoir
A Comfortable Boy

The Splendour Falls

Introduction

My father majored in English at Vanderbilt. For a course with John Crowe Ransom, Father memorized three hundred lines of poetry. Today English studies are often ephemeral. Instead of being appreciated for itself and pressed fondly into memory, literature is often read to buttress the theoretical. In Father's day books were not depots of social and political cannon fodder. In 1929 Father left Vanderbilt with a transcript of B's and C's and with an abiding love of verse. Often after riding the bus home from work, Father sat in the living room and recited poetry. The measured sounds mended ravels in the sleeve of ordinary living. "Just listen to this, Sammy," he said sitting in an armchair, stretching the kinks out of his long legs and the longer day. His great love was Tennyson, and frequently he recited songs from "The Princess," his favorite being:

> The splendour falls on castle walls
> And snowy summits old in story:
> The long light shakes across the lakes,
> And the wild cataract leaps in glory.
> Blow, bugle, blow, set the wild echoes flying,
> Blow bugle; answer, echoes, dying, dying, dying.

Father was a natural teacher. He would have been wonderful in class, and one evening I asked him why he hadn't become a teacher. "No, Sammy," he said. "I wasn't a good student. I had three jobs and worked my way through college. I didn't have any money, and besides no university would have admitted me to graduate school." I am my Daddy's son, and in this book I quote a goodly bit of poetry. Much of the poetry is first-rate, but much is also dreadful. My friend Josh says that I have replaced St. Valentine as the patron of poor versifiers. I am not sure why bad poetry attracts me. Mother may be to blame. As a girl she grew up on horseback. After she married Father she stopped riding. As the old saying puts it, you can take the girl off the horse, but you can't take the horse out of the girl. And every once in a while Mother whinnied and kicked up her verbal heels. Of course family inclination may have nothing to do with my fondness for poor poetry. Perhaps in literature as in the typical American's intimate life, a man begins his marriages with good taste and ends with bad. No matter the reason for my liking, though, my fancies are known, and readers mail me sheaves of forgettable verse. Last month a man in Missouri sent me a stanza he found printed in a newspaper lining a trunk in his attic.

> Cold water is the best of drinks, the temperance poet sings.
> But who am I that I should have the very best of things?
> Let princes revel at the pump, let saints rejoice in tea,
> Whiskey, or wine, or even beer is good enough for me.

"The accepted routine of life's conduct tends to make mountebanks of us," James Branch Cabell wrote in *Beyond Life*, adding that "the laborious years weave small hypocrisies like cobwebs about our every action, and at last about our every thought." "The reason the Dead do not return nowadays," Hilaire Belloc stated, "is the boredom of it." I never thought, as the saying puts it, that I would live long enough to make old bones. Writing like running is not as easy for the aged as it is for the young. Snipping cobwebs takes effort and strains mind and body, as does breathing life into paragraphs so that the weary don't waste their nights watching windbags huff across television.

The thoughts of diligent, creative people are always second or third hand, the results of spending hours roaming and studying. Only the lazy profess originality which, as Kingsley Loomis put it, is "inevitably a euphemism for foolishness." To keep readers interested I lean upon the "pre-owned" and quote a great deal. "In all ages," William Mathews wrote in the nineteenth century, "the greatest literary geniuses have been the greatest borrowers. Omnivorous devourers of books…they have not scrupled to seize and to turn to account every good thought they could pick up in their readings." In addition to borrowing I stray from the actual. "Memories are more permanent than fantasies, but fantasies are more important," a student said to me recently, adding, "I remember people I have made up better than real people." Mature readers realize that authors are mountebanks, especially writers of nonfiction who weave lies into nets in hopes of capturing truths. I am broad-minded and tolerate all sorts of literary shenanigans, particularly my own. The patriarchs were not so tolerant. In the *Apocrypha*, Lamech damned people who treated truth cavalierly, saying their lips were unclean, and their words "wanton and mincing as they go, tinkling." "Better to put thy hand over the hole of an asp than harken to corrupters." Like opening "a cage of evil birds," the words of such people poisoned the heart, causing the "hay to wither away and the plough to be broken."

The imagination can intoxicate and lead astray, but Lamech's jeremiad is too zealous for my palate, and page, smacking of the underbred and the under-read. Lamech assumed that words shaped deeds. The truth is that words slip out of mind as quickly as leaves tumble from sight in autumn. Moreover, influence can rarely be predicted. Last spring I received an e-mail inviting recipients to participate in a zombie movie being filmed by a graduate student. I convinced Vicki that we'd make lively zombies, "not needing much makeup," I said.

Although the e-mail blanketed the campus, Vicki and I were the only people over thirty who appeared at the tryout. A month later an article in the *Hartford Courant* described the film. Accompanying the article was a picture of Vicki and me festooned in gore. During the following week four or five people mentioned the article to me. By the weekend the article had vanished from conversation, and Vicki's and my acting careers were over. Quickly the film slipped from mind, at least until last month. On Thanksgiving I received a letter from a man who graduated from the University of Connecticut in 1991. I had been his academic advisor. He said that he reckoned he drove me "a little nuts." Anyway, he continued, I wanted to send you a greeting, writing, "When I was in Afghanistan, my mom mailed me a newspaper photo of you and your wife. You were in a zombie film. We were having a rough time of it in Helmand and Kandahar provinces and the photo of my old professor reminded me of simpler times in Storrs."

Because I have spent 94% of my years in classrooms as a student or teacher, school doings appear on my pages. Often strangers contact me about teaching. On Tuesday a man wrote declaring that he aspired to be a "transformational educator." I replied that instead of attempting to label himself he should work at being interesting. I did not point out that he'd misspelled *aspire*, inserting an extra *s* after the *a*. Actually a touch of the donkey helps teachers succeed. In the classroom braying, as the National Association of University Professors points out, is a remarkably effective "pedagogical tool."

Frequently I quote students. In his final paper, Sean described a pond in the shallows of which stood a "long-legged blue heroine." Yesterday morning when I jogged the temperature was nineteen degrees, and if the heroine were still in the pond, she'd have been blue even if she were wearing a thick down parka. Of course in Grade D paperback novels, long-legged heroines are mitteny, warming sights, usually discovered nesting in pink boudoirs. The course Sean took with me was "American Nature Writing." In this book I saunter a signature of pages studying wood and field. Often I describe birds. To an extent I think like John Burroughs. "That I am a saner, healthier, more contented man, with truer standards of life, for all my loiterings in the fields and woods, I am fully convinced," Burroughs testified in "The Gospel of Nature." "That I am less social, less interested in my neighbors and in the body politic, more inclined to shirk civic and social responsibilities and to stop my ears against the bawling of the reformers, is perhaps equally true." I don't shirk domestic responsibilities, but the body politic doesn't interest me.

Andrew Barton was a Scottish privateer beheaded in 1511 after a battle with Edward Howard and his brother. Early in the fight Barton was wounded, and according to the "Ballad of Sir Andrew Barton" said, "I'll lay me down and bleed awhile, / And then I'll rise and fight again." Although I often disappear into the woods around Storrs and frequently retire to the basement of the university library, I am not as private as Burroughs. I'm a mild Barton. After walking alone for a time or sitting in a dark nook reading, I'm soon up and fidgeting. In this book, I write about summers in Nova Scotia, vacations in the Caribbean, and visits to Tennessee. I also describe little jaunts around northeastern Connecticut. At the end of November local artists opened their studios to visitors. One Saturday Vicki and I drove to Woodstock and ate lunch in Mrs. Bridges' Pantry. We split a curried chicken sandwich and a steak and mushroom pie. Afterward we visited six home galleries. For the first year in a while we didn't buy a painting. Our walls are cluttered and our pocketbook almost bare. Spending a day exploring galleries and carrying nothing home except a fist of sentences made me worry that gusto had leached out of our days. Consequently on the drive back to Storrs we stopped in South Woodstock at Meb's Kitchenwares, and Vicki bought a wooden butter spreader, sliced from curly maple and costing twelve dollars. "This is dandy. What a good day," Vicki said as she turned the spreader in her hands, the silky surface of the wood rumpling then flaring into cool thin flames. Recollection of the day reminds me that I write a lot about domestic doings. Vicki and I laugh, but we also squabble. Occasionally the squabbles resemble run-on sentences and leap the bounds of period and paragraph because, as William Gerhardie put it of himself and his wife, we "are really so fond of each other as to express a constant and irritating solicitude as to the other's welfare."

Books are sometimes called dried tongues. When pages become arid, I sprinkle puns across them. Few people enjoy puns as much as I do. As I cannot limit myself to one potato chip at a sitting, so I am unable to restrict myself to a single pun. "Epitaphs always make me think of vegetables," a man said to his friend. "Of course," the friend replied, "they are tomb mottos." "Did you hear that an Exhibition of Incas has opened in New York?" a woman remarked. "Good Lord, what next?" her companion exclaimed, "a Show of Pen Wipers?" To balance the puns or perhaps to atone for them, I force aphorisms into my essays. "If the good die young, what the old say doesn't matter," "The punctual man wastes a lot of time waiting for other people," and "Biting off more than you can chew is harmless; attempting to swallow it is dangerous." I am also susceptible to enthusiasms. Because essays are short, indulging any interest beyond the moment is impossible. In October I thought about scarpology, the science of telling a person's character by analyzing his shoes. After considerable cogitation, however, I have concluded that wingtip shoes do not lift people into the blue ether of imagination. Instead wingtips clip the fancy, revealing that their wearers have become careerists, corporate and earthbound.

    I tell many stories in this book. Most are page-worn. I include them because they make me smile and, in fact, appreciate living. A goodly number of the tales are hokey, and for years I have placed them in Carthage, Tennessee where my great-grandfather settled after the Civil War. Prodromus McBee, I learned last month, attended Sewanee. After graduation he moved to New York and never returned to Carthage. "Prodromus caught a diploma at college and never got over it," his sister Vester said. Schooling affected Prodromus's speech, transforming the long, ocular i's in night, light, and nice into short vowels, in effect blinding them. "And," Vester said, "he had his goiter removed. For generations every McBee has had a goiter and been proud of it. Folks around Carthage call goiters the McBee coat of arms. Goiters and turnips, tobacco, and chickens that wipe their feet before they come into the house are what make us McBees famous."

    I especially like forgotten history. At the Battle of Camlann, for example, King Arthur fought Mordred's forces. Mordred was killed outright and Arthur mortally wounded. Only three of Arthur's knights survived the battle: Sandde Angel-Form who was so beautiful that Mordred's warriors believed he had come down from heaven and refused to attack him; Morfran who had hair longer than a stag and who was so ugly that people thought him a demon, and the "dusky hero of the mighty grasp," Glewlwyd Gavaelvawr, Arthur's porter, who had massive thighs and was terrifyingly strong. Some tales I repeat are instructive. In order to make a Spanish nobleman repent on his deathbed, a confessor, John Selden recounted in his *Table-Talk*, described the tortures the Devil inflicted on sinners condemned to Hell. "I hope my Lord the Devil is not so cruel," the nobleman said. When the confessor rebuked him for calling the Devil "my

Lord," the nobleman responded, saying excuse me "for calling him so. I know not into what hands I may fall, and if I happen into his, I hope he will use me the better for giving him good words."

Essayists are temporizers, not ardent believers, and resemble the nobleman more than his confessor. The risks we take are verbal, and even these are more suggestive than actual. "It is not the essayist's duty to inform, to build pathways through metaphysical morasses, to cancel abuses, any more than it is the duty of the poet to do these things," Alexander Smith wrote. The essay lies somewhere along the road between accident and design, in my case probably closer to design. Although I do not eradicate abuses or construct pathways across high seriousness to reformation, I hope my writings awaken appreciation and, if I can be mawkish, maybe love. In *Autumn Leaves*, Samuel Gardner said that integrity was "a principle of the moral sentiments quickened into life and action by the warmth of the heart." Just so or almost just so—I don't write in a fever, but writing quickens my feelings.

On the day I heard from my former advisee who had served in Afghanistan, I received a letter from a literary society, inviting me to have my portrait painted. The portrait would become part of a rogue's gallery of scribblers. A week later the artist selected by the society wrote me. He said he planned to depict me holding a book on the spine of which would appear not a title but "a motto or phrase" important to me. I haven't decided whether or not to agree to the society's request. I am not the bouncing lad I used to be, and the society wants me to appear, to quote the gospel song, "just as I am, without one plea." My teeth are yellow, and my hair is thin. I have a turkey neck, and my ears look like tubas. The talk of old men, Thomas Overbury wrote in his *Characters*, "is as terrible as their resemblance. They become wrinkled with frowning and facing youth; they admire their old customs, even to the point of eating red herring and going wetshod." If I accede to the society's wishes, I'll have "Red Herring and Wetshod" painted on the book in my hands. That will be a puzzler, or maybe not, for the surest sign of age is incomprehensibility.

The world would be safer if people read more and did less. I do not know if reading this book will better lives. But I hope that a goodly number of people read it. Nevertheless, if my readership is select, that's all right because as Vernon Lee said, "books, to fulfill their purpose, do not always require to be read." The book which is a present "has already served its purpose, like a visiting card or a luggage label." How exciting it would be to board a flight for Amsterdam or Paris, Moscow or Shanghai, and see rows of suitcases, all with copies of *The Splendour Falls* tied to the handles or pasted on the sides. Vicki says the chances of that happening are slim. What will happen, however, is that people will continue to send me stanzas of wondrously terrible verse. A moment ago Vicki handed me today's mail. One letter contained a memorable bacterial quatrain.

> Where are you going, my pretty maid?
> I'm going to sneeze, kind sir, she said.
> At whom will you sneeze, my pretty maid?
> Atchoo, atchoo, kind sir, she said.

In the Evening

Some nights after dinner, I sit alone in the study. I don't switch the lights on. I huddle in the dark and mull things. Often I think about writing. Leslie Stephen began an essay in *The Cornhill Magazine* in 1869 with an anecdote: "Mr. Creech, it is said, wrote on the margin of the *Lucretius* which he was translating, 'Mem.—when I have finished my book, I must kill myself,' and he carried out his resolution." I haven't reached this bleak stage of writing yet, but I wouldn't mind stretching out in the sun and playing dead for a day or two. Happy is the man who goes to sleep and doesn't awaken, says an old proverb, from my perspective especially the man who escapes waking up to pencils and paper and running worms of paragraphs. For years I have said, "When I finish this manuscript I am going to quit scribbling." My family, however, are taskmasters and won't let me stop picking literary oakum. They ask, "What will you do then? You don't have hobbies. You'll have a breakdown, and we will have to send you to the bughouse to be fumigated." Not until an undertaker pats me on the face with a shovel will I cease being a "biblioklept" plundering aged books and unraveling loose anecdotes.

One dissatisfaction brings another to mind. After pondering writing, I often parse my character. Because I become impatient quickly, I frequently don the jester's cap and behave foolishly. "What do you think of the color?" a woman said turning toward me in Ocean State Job Lot last Saturday, a green plaid table cloth in her hands. "Oh," she then said, "I thought you were my husband." "Madame," I said, "I have been the occasional husband of many women, but I am not your husband—at least not now." "You're a piece of work," Vicki said, pulling me away and down an aisle, pinching the triceps on my left arm. "Look at this," she continued, handing me a pillow made in India, a gecko two feet long, clothed in paisley, and with big goggle eyes. Ocean State is a hippodrome of excitement in comparison to the men's locker room at the university. "Fellows," I said on Tuesday, observing three faculty members taking showers, "You won't believe this, but yesterday I saw a naked man in the shower." "One with no clothes on," I continued before they could speak. "Not anything! Not even a necktie!" I said, my voice rising to a yelp.

On Thursday pipes in the building housing the English Department became plugged, and plumbers strung tape across the doors leading into the lavatories. The tape was yellow, and printed on it in black letters was the word *Caution*. I snipped a bit from a door. By attaching scotch tape to each end I fashioned a headband plastering *Caution* across my forehead. Afterward I roamed the building. Faculty members did not mention the headband when I strolled past. In class I advised students to study the tape, saying that the most dangerous thing in the building was the human mind. Two nodded, and at the end of period a boy asked if he could have the headband, but most of the class looked puzzled. Liveliness in a teacher does not mean that students will be lively. Still, I prefer the society of fools to that of the learned, even if I'm the only member of the former society. The conversation of the learned is often so informative that it clumps heavy on the mind much as oatmeal does in the stomach after breakfast. A batter of sermons, commonplaces, and the obvious obscurely expressed, learned conversation rarely rises to the airy magic of misunderstanding. After listening to a colorful sermon describing the tortures sinners suffered in Hell, a countryman in the congregation, Augustus Jessopp recounted, turned to his wife. "No, Sally," the man said referring to the sufferers, "it won't do. No constitution could stand it."

Many of my acquaintances have broken down and are ailing. "Waiting to have their tickets punched so they can board the Boneyard Special," my friend Josh said. Escaping pondering mortality, if only for a day, is impossible. One evening in late October I looked at my e-mail before settling into my chair. "I have JOYOUS news," I read. "Daddy has moved to a New Home. He has a New Body. Jesus is his New Best Friend. He is very Happy, and I know he will be cheering for Alabama this Saturday. Roll Tide!" The daughter of a man whom I had not thought about in forty-five years wrote the e-mail, announcing her father's death. The mail had traveled up the trunk of an electronic tree and spread along distant branches with more twigs than a weeping willow. The woman's prose startled me. As a child I learned that the simple was elegant. "Unless you are being humorous," Mother told me, "you should write *died* and *death*." The woman's phrasing did not hold my attention long. Moods of ponderers are often short-lived, and instead of considering the dead man, I started thinking about his new home. I wondered about the furnishings. Were the chairs and sideboard in the dining room Sheraton, square backed and straight-lined? Maybe the table was a Duncan Phyfe lyre-shaped pedestal table. Was there a tall case clock in the hall? Perhaps there were no clocks in the whole house, as time did not matter much in eternity. Was the plumbing modern? Or maybe homes in the golden suburbs did not need DWV Systems, the new bodies of their inhabitants being configured differently from the old bodies that soiled the earth.

For a moment I wondered what the man died from, suspecting a putrid athletic fever, but then a story came to mind, shifting my thought. Once a year in a small town, people left their houses and congregated in front yards. Hospitals and sick rooms opened their doors, and relatives and friends led the halt and the lame, all the invalids and the sick along the streets. The parade paused before each house in hopes that the inhabitants might be able to diagnose a puzzling disease or suggest remedies where doctors had failed. "About the percentage of cures effected no word remains," C. E. Montague wrote. "But some of the patients may have survived for a time." I remembered the story because endings were on my mind. Soon I will retire. I will miss students. Their writing delights me. Because they are too young to genuflect before caution tape, they take intellectual and emotional risks. Once I retire, my life will shrink, almost as if I were suffering from a wasting disease. In class this fall, students read A. M. Holmes's story "Things You Should Know." On the day in fourth grade when her teacher passed out information sheets listing "Things You Should Know," the main character was absent, at home suffering from an ear ache. As a result she did not receive the list and throughout life kept stumbling over things other people knew but which she did not know. I asked students to make up sheets listing things that they missed and wish they had been told. "Don't tell your family you are gay on Thanksgiving," Robert wrote. "Why hasn't someone taught me how to walk through wet grass in high heels?" Julienne asked. "Before I applied to college, I wish I had known," Brian wrote, "that the best way to appear confident is not to care about what you are doing."

Student essays are endlessly entertaining. "I did not have an imaginary friend when I was little," Emilia wrote. "Instead I pretended someone identical to me lived on the other side of the globe. The girl had to do what I did at exactly the same time. I entertained myself by thinking up silly things for her to do. I imagined her laughing when our invisible connection forced her to hop about squawking like a chicken or made her turn cartwheels across her front yard until she rolled into a pile of leaves her father had raked. As I grew older, this notion expanded and the number of beings identical to me multiplied. Eventually there were hundreds, living on all the planets in our solar system and in fabulous, undiscovered worlds. Because so many me's existed and followed my instructions, I thought that once I grew up and learned how serious things worked—tides and temperature, rain and snow—that I would be able to shape the future. I realized the responsibility was great. But my mother and father were nice people. They were raising me well, and I hoped I'd behave properly."

Emilia's whimsy will lighten her future. In contrast Jesse is an odd stick, and I worry that he won't thrive planted in conventional society. His thought, however, has quickened my evenings. "I cannot imagine trees see the world the way humans do," he wrote recently. "They must look at weeks and years like we look at hours and days. A person would have to spend a month with a tree before it noticed him. Sometimes I envy trees. The feeling of morning sunlight on a thousand leaves must be superior to any natural pleasure a human can enjoy. No longer do I think that trees can help me get closer to God or judge the quality of my life. It seems impossible that their wisdom is comparable to what humans call wisdom. But still I would like to know their opinions about things. Their memories must be wonderful....I read about an ecosystem in South America in which the trees and all other plants share roots. As a result a tree responds to a stimulus centered miles away. Trees probably know each other even when they are not connected in this manner. After a score of years I imagine that an oak and a maple develop an understanding of each other and share the experience of their forest in some quiet, physical way." I shouldn't fret about Jesse. He has a touch of the poetic in his nature, and he'll have a good, green life. Moreover, as Emerson reassuringly put it in "Society and Solitude," "We pray to be conventional. But the wary Heaven takes care you shall not be, if there is anything good in you."

Students are often curious about things that seem absurd to adults. "I wore my watch upside down today," Sarah recounted. Sarah had put her watch on in the dark and busy with finishing a lab report did not notice the watch for an hour. She resisted the "urge to fix its position" and decided to keep it upside down for the rest of the day. "Perhaps," she mulled, "I approached this as a simple thought experiment: whether or not I could function not knowing the right time or whether I could tolerate having something within my control being imperfect and untidy." I hoped, she continued, the experiment would reveal "deep personality patterns" or "bring to light aspects of my character that lay dormant smothered by schedule." At the end of the day, she wrote, she adjusted her watch, having reached that most satisfactory of all conclusions "nothing." "I wondered what the purpose of wearing it upside down had been, and why I took such delight every time that I happened to look down and remember that my watch was inverted." Routine deadens thought, and sometimes, especially during long gray afternoons, I imagine climbing onto the roof of my house, wrapping myself around the chimney as if it were a mast, and shouting, "Help, man over-bored!" In part student papers are rafts. Their quirky imbalance restores balance and helps keep me buoyant—sane and contented.

I have not retired because I worry that I haven't saved enough money to care for Vicki in her dotage. Sometimes I mull "get rich quick" schemes. Recently I thought about a banana manufactory. A banana shucking machine needs to be invented. After bananas are shucked, the edible fingers can be crushed. To add color and squeeze publicity from glitzy magazines like *Condé Nast Traveler*, I'd hire actors, primarily bulbous females, to impersonate "natives" and dance barefoot atop the fingers, pulping them as if they were grapes, transforming the process into a frenchified "folknik effusion." Bananas could then be shipped by the cask and not by the stalk, saving cargo space in refrigerator ships and also protecting consumers from the occasional spider or viper hiding amid the stalks. Later grocery stores would sell the "meat" using squidgy machines similar to those which dispense natural peanut butter. Customers would fill plastic tubs with the meat and later serve it by the spoonful. Plans that glow in the dark lose their glitter in the light. "The meat will turn brown," Vicki said when I described the scheme. "Soft brown bananas are icky, and people won't buy the meat." Vicki is good with financial matters, so I jettisoned my plan. This year she paid only $2.08 for our Thanksgiving turkey. At Stop & Shop customers who bought twenty-five dollars worth of food were eligible to purchase frozen turkeys for fifty-eight cents a pound. Vicki bought a twelve and two-tenths pound turkey, the price being $7.08. In a flyer Stop & Shop advertised, "We will match any competitor's turkey coupon." Vicki had a five dollar coupon from Big Y. When the coupon was applied to the purchase, the price fell to $2.08.

 Vicki can be entertainingly bossy, and after dinner I often think about the "Rules of Engagement." The rules regulate my domestic doings. I, for example, own two pairs of slippers, an indoor and an outdoor pair. The rules dictate that when I get out of bed in the morning I put on the indoor pair and wear them downstairs to the kitchen. Once in the kitchen, I take off the indoor slippers and put on the outdoor slippers, after which I open the back door and let the dogs out. I walk thirty yards to the end of the driveway and fetch the paper. I then return to the house and let the dogs back in. Once I am in the kitchen again, I take off the outdoor slippers and put on the indoor slippers. Although not as complicated as the income tax code, slipper rules are complex. Shuffling the feet is forbidden, something that comes natural to the slipper wearer.

Our kitchen is tiny. The sink and surrounding counter are near the refrigerator. If I support myself on the counter using my left hand, plaster my left foot flat on the floor and hold the refrigerator door open with a right, slippered foot, I can remove milk for my cereal from the lower shelf in the refrigerator with my right hand, pour the milk into a cereal bowl on the counter, then replace the milk container without letting the door shut. This maneuver raises my spirits. It reassures me that I still have a sense of balance, and it is environmentally friendly using practically no energy. Nevertheless it is forbidden. "Holding a door open with a foot is unsanitary," Vicki has said, ignoring my contention that I always wear clean, indoor slippers when I execute the maneuver. Other rules regulate parking the car. Although I have never dented a bumper and Vicki has had four fender banging incidents, all in parking lots, I am not allowed to switch the ignition off until after she has circumnavigated the car and made sure I have parked in the center of a space, far enough away from other vehicles so their doors cannot whack us.

Rules exist to be broken, and I am constitutionally disobedient, especially when it comes to cookie tins. Vicki is a wonderful cook and every month bakes cookies. She piles the cookies into tins then hides the tins. When I was a child, I imagined becoming a famous explorer, roaming the globe and making golden discoveries. Although domestic responsibilities have kept me close to home, bound to gutters and lawn mowers, tuition and pediatricians, I still hanker to explore. Whenever Vicki cooks a batch of cookies, I put the hankering to practical use. No matter how craftily Vicki hides the tins, Vasco Da Gama Pickering discovers them. Moreover, I have a bit of Admiral Parry in me. Filching from the tins so that Vicki won't notice cookies have vanished takes skill, and I have become expert at constructing cookie igloos. I am able to remove cookies from the bottoms of tins without causing the piles of cookies to sink, thus maintaining the illusion that the tin has remained undiscovered, its contents an untouched gustatory treasure.

The rules regulating eating cookies are strict. Vicki allows me one cookie for dessert at dinner. Two weeks ago she baked chocolate chip cookies. The cookies were voluptuous, nippled with big, soft chips. After I ate my single allotted cookie, Vicki broke another cookie in half. "It is not good for you," she said, "but you can have half this cookie." "I don't want it," I said, admiring my own restraint. "Yes, you do," Vicki said. "Now take it." "I don't want it," I repeated. "Put it back in the tin." "No, you want it," she said. "Eat it. But don't ask for any more." "I don't want it," I said. "Of course, you want it," Vicki answered. "This shilly-shallying around is angering me. Eat this cookie and be quiet and don't even think about asking for another cookie, Fatso." "Fatso?" I said, reaching for the cookie; "That's no way to address the Shakespeare of Storrs." "Shakespeare? Falstaff fits you better, fat and red-faced with caution tape wrapped around his forehead. Now eat the cookie and go to your study," Vicki said closing the tin and shooing me out of the kitchen. A great explorer must break rules and occasionally act contrary. Balboa Pickering obeyed and left the kitchen, but he shuffled. Once in the study, I considered putting on outdoor slippers, but I realized the act was too revolutionary—the sort of deed that undermines the social edifice.

I don't always sit in the dark. Last week I turned on the lights and imagined turning the study into a conservatory. Instead of hot house plants, I cultivated the homey plants of wayside and yard: violets and clovers, bugle and gill, baneberry, wild pinks, and star flowers. Jack preached from his pulpit, but he didn't rail. Bachelors wore their buttons, but they did not rule out the possibility of marriage. Cleomes doused themselves with minty aftershave, and nasturtiums hid their peppery natures behind wide orange smiles. I feasted on butter-and-eggs and drank the sweet unpasteurized fragrance of milkweed. For story's sake I planted Hyacinths. According to myth, Hyacinth was a beautiful young Spartan. Both Apollo and Zephyrus, god of the west wind, fell in love with him. Zephyrus became viciously jealous when Hyacinth rejected him and chose Apollo as a lover. One day Zephyrus came upon Hyacinth and Apollo when they were throwing the discus. Zephyrus swept the discus up in a gust of wind and blew it into Hyacinth's skull, killing him. Apollo was grief-stricken, and as a memorial created a purple flower using drops of Hyacinth's blood. I considered planting other flowers associated with myths, Narcissus for example. But in the harsh lamp light, I remembered something Thomas De Quincey wrote. "Of all the bores," De Quincey opined, "whom man in his folly hesitates to hang, and Heaven in its mysterious wisdom suffers to propagate his species, the most insufferable is the teller of good stories."

The flowers I cultivated bloomed in spring and summer. The sky outside the study was wintry, and the conservatory conceit wilted. Moreover two hours had passed since dinner, and the time had come to put the dogs out, a duty the rules assigned to me. A smidgen of canine runs through the blood of all men. Night heats the blood of males slightly. Men generally don't bay or howl, but if a man puts a dog outside, he accompanies his pal around the yard. "A friend was fined two hundred dollars for peeing in the woods near the campus one night," my student Chris told me, adding, "and I think he was put on a list of the sexually felonious." Normal males who own dogs and who are required to walk them in the evening always "visit" the woods with their animals, even males who live beside busy thoroughfares as I do. The only exception to visiting occurs during full moon, a time I have come to dislike, agreeing with Logan Pearsall Smith. "And then one night, low above the trees, we saw the great amorous, unabashed face of the full moon," Smith wrote in *All Trivia*. "It was an exhibition that made me blush, feel that I had no right to be there. 'After all these millions of years, she ought to be ashamed of herself!' I cried."

G. K. Chesterton entitled one of his books *All Is Grist*. When I return to the study after putting the dogs out, I leave the light on and read. My reading ranges haphazardly, and almost everything becomes grist worth ruminating over. Last night I read Robert Lynd's collection of essays *The Green Man*. In "Fair Play for Man," Lynd discussed harvesting organs from apes in order to extend the life of man. After noting that no ape had ever "torn" glands from a man to rejuvenate itself, he wrote, "There is no reason to suppose that the self-denial of apes in this matter, so fortunate for ourselves, is prompted by motives of humanity. The ape is an animal less clever than ourselves, and, if it spares us and our glands, this is due, not to any tenderness for us, but to its abysmal ignorance. Let the apes but go to school for a few centuries, and devote themselves to research work at their universities, and we shall find them experimenting on human beings as callously as human beings have ever experimented on animals. And why should they not? Naturally, they think that the world was made for apes, and that it is better that a hundred human beings should perish than that one ape should suffer a headache."

Voices

Turn the Master's radio on, the gospel song urges. "Get in touch with God" and "listen to the music in the air." Before promoters jammed airwaves and drowned out heavenly messages with corporate static, getting in touch with God was easy. "The Works of this visible world," John Ray wrote in 1691, afforded "a demonstrative Proof of the unlimited extent of the Creators Skill, and the fecundity of his Wisdom and Power." Although God has vanished from the contemporary visible world, many people wander nature, searching not for belief or dogma, but in hopes of awakening feelings and invigorating their moral sensibilities. Others search for mercy, praying that encounters with leaves and petals will bestow momentary forgetfulness upon them, enabling them to escape the dreary secular voices of buying and selling. Two days ago after a dry morning of grading papers, I walked the Fenton River. The banks were gardens of trout lilies, wood anemones, winy wake Robin, and violets, sweet white, yellow, and northern bog, these last dark blue muffs hugging the ground. Yesterday blue birds flew the fence line bracketing the pasture behind Horsebarn Hill, and yellow warblers hung like small bright lanterns on grey dogwood above a marsh. In a frolic of mating toads beat the shallows of Beaver Pond into froth, and last night I chased a great horned owl from a perch in the side yard in hopes of keeping her from wiping out a family of flying squirrels nesting in a broken black birch.

In March after the men's basketball team at the University of Connecticut won the national championship, I met the athletic director on campus. "Sam, long time, no see," he said, then exclaimed, "a great day for the Husky Nation" (the husky dog being the university's mascot). Before I could reply, the man had hurried past, greeting another faculty member, the only phrase I heard being "Husky Nation," the words a hallelujah, part of a corporate anthem. Before people worshipped temporalities like athletics, theological voices were not so stale. In 1794, John Berridge tutored a friend on the art of itinerant preaching. "When you open up your commission," Berridge wrote, "begin with ripping up the audience, and Moses will lend you a carving knife, which may often be whetted at his grind-stone....Declare the evil of sin in its effects, bringing all our sickness, pains, and sorrows, all the evils we feel, and all the evils we fear:—All inundations, fire, famines, pestilences, brawls, quarrels, fightings, wars,—with death, these present sorrows,—and Hell to receive all that die in sin." "You must wave," Berridge concluded, "the Gospel Flag, and magnify the Saviour proudly; speak with a full mouth, that his blood can wash away the foulest stains, and his grace subdue the stoutest corruptions."

Today many people would not understand Berridge's words. Actually they would also be mystified by George Jean Nathan's remarks on immortality. "The doctrine of the afterlife," Nathan wrote in *Land of the Pilgrims' Pride*, "as expounded by the rev. clergy, is based upon the optimistic theory that if the cook drops a cheap china soup-plate, breaks it into a hundred pieces and lets them lie on the floor long enough, they will shortly, after the mistress of the house has stopped crying, resynthesize themselves in the form of a beautiful Sèvres vase." In April I read Uncle Remus's account of the Tar Baby to one of my classes. Afterward I asked the class to name the book in which the story appeared. "The Bible," Stephanie shouted. "That," I said, "is the most asinine answer I've heard in 45 years of teaching. Hallelujah!"

Because students are not attuned to the cymbals of biblical and folk tales does not, of course, mean they lack distinctive voices. "I believe in time, or at least abide by it," Julia wrote. "Time is difficult to break away from even when I don't have to be somewhere. I believe in timeless moments which may or may not be necessary in a time-constrained world. I believe in these moments because time is only an invention. All manmade conceptions are the same. They make our lives run quicker and with minimal thought. I believe in these inventions and use them because they are there, but they are not necessary for existence. For example, I believe in microwaves and use them often, but I also believe in microwavelessness. After all, some things are better cold." "I am not sure whether you said a lot or said nothing," I wrote at the end of Julia's paper. "But I enjoyed the essay, and the enjoyable always deserves praise."

Near the end of the semester Mary described trying to save the life of a starling fledgling she found on a road. The bird died, and Mary cried, after which she compared her attitude toward death to that of her mother. "My mother," she wrote, "is a nurse in the Intensive Care Unit of a large hospital. Despite all the plaques and Christmas ornaments that claim nurses are the heart of healthcare, angels in comfortable shoes, the truth—which is not to say that all the cross-stitched quotations are erroneous—is that the perspective of nurses on life and death differs from that of many people. While some folks flip to the comics in the morning, my mother opens to the obituaries. 'Oh, look,' she will say in a tone most people reserve for discussing the weather. 'There's Mr. Alan. He was a nice man.' Our refrigerator is covered with novelty magnets, childhood pictures, PTA flyers, and long strips of newspaper, obituaries for strangers. Mother thinks them interesting, a life summed up in a single clichéd announcement. Who went before, who was left behind, where he worked, how many children he had."

Like Mary's mother I paste obituaries on the refrigerator. Often as I read an obituary, I scroll through my past, and I hear forgotten voices. Recently I thought about the mother of a friend who when her daughter mentioned an acquaintance from a suspect family invariably said, "We don't know them," the emphasis falling on *don't* and *them*, the pronunciation of this last word magically curling up into contempt while simultaneously flattening down into dismissal. As a person ages, funereal and medical matters become increasingly interesting. This past Monday while Vicki endured a ward of optical tests at the Massachusetts Eye and Ear Infirmary, I roamed halls, studying cases of medical instruments. I coveted a pair of iron spectacles dating from 1790 and heavy-duty enough to withstand the tumbles I take trailing birds through scrub. Eye stones had less appeal. Comparatively flat and about the size of a raisin, a stone was "placed in the inner corner of the eye and allowed to work its way out removing a foreign body at the same time." Tonsillotomes or Tonsil Splitters were the prizes of the otolaryngology collection, this including mouth gags and mastoid gouges. One tonsillotome looked like a small dinner setting consisting of a fork and forceps while another replaced the forceps with a diminutive guillotine, sharp enough to allow doctors to forgo all tenderizers.

Generally voice refers to literary matters: syntax, diction, and pronunciation, among others. Form influences voice, Hemingway's short sentences and Faulkner's endless serpentine paragraphs, patternless free verse or the hand clapping rhythm and slap of the heroic couplet, an example being Dryden's "In pious times, ere priest-craft did begin, / Before polygamy was made a sin; / When man, on many, multipl'd his kind, / Ere one to one was cursedly confin'd." For my part, preachy voices appeal to me, their contents lozenges soothing their stuffiness. "It is not, then, how much a man may know that is of importance," Samuel Smiles wrote in *Self-Help*, "but the end and purpose for which he knows it. The object of knowledge should be to mature wisdom and improve character, to render us better, happier, and more useful; more benevolent, more energetic, and more efficient in the pursuit of every high purpose in life."

No longer am I the incensed librarian's fiery fellow traveler. Time has doused the embers of literary fervor. My spirits have cooled, and in my dotage, voices of bemused common sense attract me more than cries of outrage. "As one grows older one finds it increasingly difficult to be interested in a book merely because it has been suppressed," Robert Lynd declared in *The Goldfish*. "Hope has so often been disappointed. I do not know what it is that we do not already know that we expect to find in books which have been put out of the way as nuisances. There can be no new words, for the worst have all been scribbled on walls already. There can be no new vices, for all the vices were invented before the Flood."

Time changes the appeal of literary voices. Never again will I watch a performance of *Othello*. I cannot trust myself to remain silent when Othello says to Desdemona, "O, ay, as summer flies are in the shambles, / That quicken even with the blowing. O thou weed, / Who art so lovely fair, and smell'st so sweet, / That the sense aches at thee, would thou hadst never been born!" "Damn it to Hell, you thick clown," I'm bound to shout. "Iago has sunk the lie into you and played you like a carp. Desdemona is innocent. She's a lamb, and if you even consider putting out the light, I will leap on stage and pound the living shit out of you." Some voices age better than others. Those seasoned with humor settle the nerves and rarely leave a bilious aftertaste. Graham Greene's *Travels with My Aunt* gallivants off the first page into laughter with Henry the main character remarking, "I have never married. I have always lived quietly, and apart from my interest in dahlias, I have no hobby. For those reasons I found myself agreeably excited by my mother's funeral." At the funeral Henry meets his Aunt Augusta, this after hearing her remark, "I was once present at a premature cremation."

Every day is a chorus of voices, a few bass and whispered, others soprano, some falsetto. Almost never do the voices blend, and the melody most frequently produced is the absence of pattern. Quips rise and fall quickly, most a cappella, "Get down on your knees and thank god you're still on your feet" or advice given to someone soon to give life the go-by, "Don't buy any green bananas," the implication being that by the time the bananas ripen the person will have handed in his breakfast bowl. The unexpected often shapes voice. In April the university was host to the Southern New England 4-H Poultry Show. "Coop In," not the expected sign or check in, ran from 8:30 until 10:30 in the morning. Not long ago a friend wrote from Dallas saying that armadillo had become a staple of local eateries, "under the stars" restaurants listing it among appetizers, labeling it "opossum on the half shell." "She doted on foreign missions and was a pious cook," Tabitha Broadmax's husband testified in her obituary in the *Memphis Commerical Appeal*. "She could fry the best piece of tripe I ever slung under my vest, and her greens never suffered from the gravel and was always toothsome." Occasionally, voices produce ripples of laughter and horror simultaneously, like the statement of an acquaintance who "surfacing" after a stroke announced, "I'm a piece of broccoli." A student in one of my classes last year wrote a tender essay describing the last year of her grandmother's life. "Grandpa," as "Grandma" referred to her husband, died some months earlier. Every Sunday the student's family took Grandma to lunch, even as the old woman's silver cord loosened, shedding knots of reason and propriety. Grandma ate heartily and for the most part silently, although at least once during the meal she laid her knife and fork aside and looking around the restaurant announced to people dining nearby that "Grandpa sure liked his pussy."

Gone is the proper voice, especially for the American female. "We expect most of our talking to be done by women," Emily Taplin wrote near the end of the nineteenth century, "and it is really necessary that our girls should practice the art. To begin with, the voice must be agreeable. Harsh tones must be modified; clearness of utterance cultivated, and one should try to attain 'a low sweet voice.'" Taplin urged women, or better perhaps ladies, to chose language carefully, making sure to avoid "vulgar catch words." "If girls knew the abominable low origin of many slang phrases that they so glibly repeat, we think they would utterly abjure them in disgust." Many other words were simply objectionable and incorrect. "Take, for example, that most terrible of all Americanisms, 'pants,'" Taplin said, noting that cultivated speakers used "trousers."

The most distinctive voice I hear is that of Vicki. During the basketball tournament that transformed the university into the Husky Nation, she asked as a sportscaster was bouncing beyond hyperbole, "How many players on the court are allowed to throw the ball at the basket?" Of our dog Suzy, she said last week, "Suzy is not a deep thinker." Occasionally Vicki scolds me. I know better than to reply, but common sense rarely influences behavior. After being criticized for wiping milk off the kitchen floor with a dishtowel, I responded, "I'm not a bad husband, and in any case I'm what you've got." "Yes," Vicki said, exhaling in resignation, "There's not enough time left to look for anything better."

Many of the loudest voices a person hears are imagined. Such voices enliven dull hours. According to Greek mythology the Sirens sang so beautifully that they enchanted sailors and lured them to their deaths. Because he wanted to hear the Sirens, Odysseus ordered his sailors to plug their ears with beeswax then bind him to the mast of his boat in order to prevent his succumbing to the songs. After they sailed out of hearing, Odysseus signaled to his shipmates by scowling, and the sailors unplugged their ears and freed him. The story quickens stale reality, in Odysseus's case the ten years spent sailing home from Troy, breasting wave after wave, or in contemporary terms, sculling through the doldrums of board or class room. Actually the Sirens were not Harpy-like, dagger-clawed women who wrecked mariners, devouring body and soul. They were neither beautiful nor ugly. They were simply a mist which men peopled or "monstered" in order to quicken their mundane lives.

Early one morning in February I drove to Gengras Volvo in East Hartford. Ice covered the interstate, turning the road's shoulders into a wrecking yard of crumpled cars. I should not have left home, but weather had made me cancel two previous appointments. While a mechanic balanced the tires on my car, I sat in a waiting room drinking black coffee, the only cream available chemical sawdust. A fog sank over East Hartford covering the windows of the garage like an eye patch. Shortly afterward I sailed beyond the room and the splintery ice outside, not thinking about Sirens but about birds, their winged cousins, compiling a field guide to promiscuous birds, excluding species that mated for life, banishing dullards like Canada geese from my paragraphs while celebrating those domestic gadabouts wrens. Later I mulled writing *A Book of Unclean Beasts* and composed a table of contents including among others, opossums, raccoons, dump chickens, dung hill rats, hairball mice, Republicans, cortex tapeworms, and that aviary of black-robed poltroons, the justices of the Supreme Court. Actually whenever weather straps me to the mast of place, I often hear Sirens and forgetting reason sail rocky imaginative waters. Last week while wind howled in a high serenade, I sketched an essay entitled "Armadillos with Leprosy." As might be expected not a single armadillo or outbreak of leprosy appeared in the essay. Instead the piece was a moving account of the birth of a firstborn son although yesterday I thought about changing it to a tearful diary describing the death then burial of a beloved mother.

In the waiting room at Gengras, I chatted with a retired florist. My grandfather was a florist, and while the man talked, my mind drifted to flowers. Flowers don't speak, but they are not silent. Bees shake through foxglove ringing blossoms like a carillon. Oriental lilies blare into notes, pink and red, white, yellow, and orange, some of the doubles drumming. While daffodils grin and make observers smile, bearded iris, especially red and blue varieties, murmur like ancient relatives, great aunts who serve Jell-O for dessert but who sometimes bake five layer yellow chocolate cakes. That afternoon in the mail, I received a catalogue of Comstock Seeds from the Wethersfield Seed Gardens. The catalogue seemed a babble of voices. Kale and collards were lowland and southern even if some folks called Ragged Jack kale Russian Red. Perkin's long pod okra was southern, too, but upland, perhaps from Appalachia, stretching the short *I* in nice and right into a long squint. Country gentleman corn had relatives who were cobblers in Connecticut. For their part hollow crown parsnips and golden ball turnips were old-fashioned, using words like *brogans* and describing the whereabouts of a manure pile by saying it was "over yonder behind the red barn." Snap beans were lively, but eggplants were dull, their speech slightly curmudgeonly and anything but purple. As could be expected potatoes were stuffy; even sweet potatoes couldn't enliven their conversation, no matter what they did for pies and custards.

In February I went to an exhibition of Thomas Lawrence's portraits at the Yale Center for British Art. Lawrence painted at the end of the eighteenth and beginning of the nineteenth century. Many of his sitters were elegant women, clothes flowing over them in quiet gray and silver washes, their skin soft bars tinged with red. Amid the beauty I became melancholy. No longer do fine paintings broaden the horizons of possibility. Instead they make me aware of lives impossible to live, even in imagination. They illustrate that the misty indulgent isle of dreams where I once spent many green, intoxicating moments has become rocky and barren, salty, an uninhabitable place that doesn't stretch the shrinking margins of living.

Words and dreams are yoked. Vocabulary creates the world. The richer one's vocabulary, the more he perceives and the more he imagines. Much as Lawrence's paintings brought awareness of loss, so the fraying of my vocabulary has changed my voice, undermining sensibility. I worry my voice has become tinny, sounding like the proverbial five cents of God-help-us. This past semester a student wrote asking to interview me. He explained that he was "a member of the Leadership Learning Community on campus," adding that he wanted to quiz me about my leadership role at the university. "I appreciate your contacting me," I replied, "but I am not a campus leader. To write a person often has to retire from others. Writers are usually observers rather than leaders. They are people who poke around. For example, I haven't met the president of the university. I do not know members of the board of trustees or any of the makers and shakers on campus." That portion of my reply was sound, but then my response turned brittle. "Over the years I have been interviewed many times, not something I find pleasant. I prefer that people read my books. The only way I will now be interviewed is by e-mail. That gives me time to think about answers and avoid silly and embarrassing spontaneity. In short I am not the person for you." If my correspondent had been a junior or senior, my note would have intrigued him, and he might have pushed harder for an interview. But he was a freshman expecting conventional enthusiasm and conviviality, and I did not hear from him again. "Shouldn't I have been warmer and more receptive?" I asked Vicki. "Are you still thinking about voice?" she asked. She did not wait for an answer, but instead stood and walked into the back yard, pausing at the screen door to quote the old saying, "You have a splendid ear but a poor voice, as the conductor said to the donkey."

Pondering one's voice can lead to the writing sin, autolaudation, so I dropped the subject. In any case I had to pack a suitcase because the next morning I was flying to Chattanooga for the biennial meeting of the Fellowship of Southern Writers. "When a traveler does not observe," the Royal Geographic Society's *Hints to Travellers* stated in 1893, "it is a loss both to himself and others." Observation is a good gargle, scrubbing the abrasive from the throat. "See you, sweetie" and "Bye-bye, darling," waitresses said when I left the Inside Restaurant in Chattanooga after eating breakfast, a trifle more affectionate than Vicki's last words at the airport in Hartford, "When did you say you'd be back?" One evening I spoke to a men's book club. The host was a urologist, his specialty the prostate. "I'm not allowed to talk about my work at dinner," he told me. "I think it really interesting, but the rest of the family," he continued then stopped, a shrug completing his thought and serving as a period.

In Chattanooga, I visited the Tennessee Aquarium and saw a host of creatures I'd never seen before, among others, lookdown fish, flat and silvery, ribs rippling their sides; peacock bass; golden-headed box turtles; yellow and blue poison dart frogs; upside-down jellyfish, their tops frizzes of white frosting, their bottoms waffles; and elephant nose fish, a ruffle of fins around their abdomens, a limber snorkel at the snout. I didn't notice as much as I hoped because I hurried through the aquarium. "Fabulous First Graders" from the Michigan Avenue School applied quirts to my step, their voices slapping through the buildings in stinging, lacerating shrieks. Twice during my stay in Chattanooga I ran the city for over two hours, on the first occasion jogging down Broad Street, crossing the Tennessee River at the Walnut Street Bridge, and then roaming North Chattanooga, the highlight of my explorations being the Coolidge Park Carousel, three rings of wooden animals. I rode the carousel twice, both rides influenced, a critic might conclude, by my visit to the aquarium. On the first ride I rode a bulbous carp with blue fins and gold scales. For the second I mounted a green frog dressed in a yellow jacket, a red and black striped necktie, khaki trousers, and brown wingtip shoes with black laces. In the right rear pocket of the frog's trousers was a wallet. Leaping was hard on the frog's clothes, and the fly on his trousers had sprung, bulging open near the waist, this last noticeable only when a person crawled under the frog, something I did because a lively woman in an antique shop said the "sight is not to be missed."

 The following morning I ran northeast beside the river along the Riverpark toward the Chickamauga Dam, turning around after reaching an industrial complex. My run began behind the houses of "the local financial Taliban," as a man referred to owners of big homes bolted to the bluff above the river. The trail eventually descended to lower fiduciary regions and wound through meadows and wetlands. Robins scooted through the grass. Swallows swerved and pirouetted, and the happy jangle of mockingbirds never stopped. A great blue heron fished a swamp, and gold finches chattered through saplings in yellow blurs. Princess trees dropped purple horns, and the fragrance of black locust hung sweet in the air like invisible smoke. For a moment I seemed to be listening to the Master's radio. The delusion quickly dissipated. Ahead of me on the lip of the path sat a bullfrog. Just as I saw the frog, a hefty girl on a bicycle raced past. When she saw the frog, she swerved and ran over it, crushing its back. "Yes," she shouted, turning back into the middle of the path and lifting her right hand from the handlebars in triumph. Two minutes later I ran past three black tanker cars on a siding. Painted in big white letters on the side of one of the cars was "God Hates Us All." "Shitfire," I said aloud, finding my voice.

    That afternoon I was part of a panel discussing politics and literature. "Why are you on this panel?" a woman in the audience asked me. "Isn't that obvious?" I replied, "Genius," the only time anyone has ever called me a genius. My voice smacked of biblical sounding brass, but it was no longer tinny. "What a marvelous discussion," a man exclaimed afterward, approaching me. "Healthy, too," he said, opening his fist exposing a brownish pebble about half the size of an eye stone. "A kidney stone," he said when I looked puzzled. "I passed this right after the panel ended." Normally I would have been speechless. But running had not only tuned but balanced my voice. "That's astonishing," I said, adding, "but here is something for you." "Can you tell me why a conundrum that nobody can solve is like a ghost?" When the man shook his head, signaling *no*, I said, "Do you want me to tell you now or two years from now when I return to Chattanooga?" On the man's replying *now*, I said, "Sooner or later everybody must give it up."

The Purposeless Life

A scrap of paper lay on the floor of the room. I leaned over and picked it up. "So sorry about running out of class!" it said. "The bus was running really late, so I decided at the last minuet to drive my car, so I wouldn't miss the quiz & now I am parked illegally!" Tom was the first student to show up for the examination, and before dropping the paper into my carryall, I read it to him, noting "Amy's" confusion of dance with time. Tom had recently read the best-seller *The Purpose Driven Life*, and he asked why I saved the paper. "I don't know," I said.

I think predestination nutty. Only rarely have I pondered a destination that lay out of sight around the curve of the next hour. "When He reached down his hand for me," the gospel song begins. Not only has no he, or she, ever reached for me, but I have rarely reached for anything. "True liberty does not consist in being able to do what we wish," an old saw preaches, "but in being able to do what we ought to wish." Aside from hoping that others experience good health and fortune, I don't know what I ought to wish for. Both Infancy and Age, the first and last pages in the Book of Life, are blank. Maybe my purposelessness merely reflects Age, Time's having erased youthful stirrings from memory.

"Half the pleasures of the woods and fields are for those who take things as they come," Robert Lynd wrote in *The Goldfish*, urging readers to toss the reins of purpose, and meandering days, enjoy the passing moment. My students finished the examination at ten. At noon I submitted final grades to the registrar. Before locking the tests in my office, I copied two sentences Luke wrote. Luke's remarks seemed prescient, restating Lynd and mirroring my mood. "Expectation is one of the most unfortunate things one can take into the world. Focusing on an end will result in a person's missing an almost infinite array of possibilities." At seven the next morning Vicki and I boarded a Delta flight in Hartford, headed for Fort Lauderdale and three weeks cruising the Caribbean on Holland America's *Maasdam*, mincing places into a paste of impressions, among others Antigua, Belize, Guatemala, St. Maarten, Honduras, and St. Thomas. Eschewing purpose slices both the past and the future from life, the former not bound to the present by cause and effect, the latter arbitrary and incapable of being influenced by goal or intention. For me now, travel consists of the thin edge of the momentary, sights that quickly flow back along blades thickening into tangs hidden beneath handles.

The "Ship of Fools" is a literary device suitable for sailing smooth, artificial pages but not a life-worthy vessel. After three weeks together passengers on the cruise ship resembled a high-school senior class, some members forever gladdening lounge and poolside, working the deck chairs in hopes of being elected president, vice-president, and bubbly secretary-treasurer. To be sure I met striking individuals: a professional golfer from the Netherlands, the engineer in charge of wiring on the space shuttle, a sociologist from Cornell who paid for scrapbooks of cruises by lecturing as a sexologist and to whom, I should add, neither Vicki nor I had much to say, a Rumanian diplomat who after the execution of the Ceausescu's moved to Venezuela and taught political science, a retired couple both of whom had worked for the CIA, and a pilot who for thirty years had flown cargo planes through the stormy weather of two score wars and revolutions. Because passengers ate meals at odd times and in different restaurants, conversation was almost always light, rarely anything other than hors d'oeuvres composed of pleasantries occasionally savory with decorative green aphorisms. Generally talk circled, subjects of sentences spinning

The Splendour Falls

around to swallow predicates like the courting talk of the fabled shy man. Hard put to think of something to say when alone in the parlor with his girl, the man asked, "How is your Ma?" On the girl's replying that her mother was well, the man then asked, "How is your Pa?" On the girl's answering that her father was also well, the man paused and rubbed his hands together in hopes of squeezing words from the palms. "Well, well," he eventually said. "That's mighty fine, mighty agreeable, and by the way while we are on the subject, how are your parents?"

Occasionally, however, talk startled. Unlike the tight-lipped CIA couple for whom nods constituted words, a woman who had retired from the State Department was garrulous, fluffing up conversational gaps with stories, some of which were robin's egg blue. Charlene and Bobby were two-year-old twins, she recounted at lunch the second day of the cruise. One afternoon while they were in their playpen, Charlene shouted, "Rape! Rape!" "For God's sake, Charlene," Bobby said in exasperation, trying to take a nap. "Chill out. Take a Valium. You are sitting on your pacifier." The woman must have been good diplomat. Her tales ranged more broadly than the *Decameron*, and she spread them across lapses in conversation, occasionally like mustard but usually like mayonnaise. Two countrymen were talking, she said, interrupting a tedious soliloquy on professional football. "The two strongest men in the olden times," one of the men said, "were Hercules and Samson." "That's fascinating," the second man said, adding, "What can you tell me about them?" "Oh," the first man answered, "Samson was a regular Hercules." "Goodness," the second man responded. "Who would have thought it?"

As the tainted usually lingers longer on the tongue than the fresh so the spoiled remark is less perishable than the amenable. In Belize City Vicki and I wanted to visit the zoo, and we asked several people if they wanted to share a taxi with us. "No," a woman botoxed out of expression said standing on the tender pier and looking into the city. "I have seen poor people in many countries. They are always unappealing. I don't need to see more of them. I'm returning to the ship." "The trouble with America," a dark outspoken man said, "is that we've got too many people voting for a living and not enough working for a living." At dinner one evening an English woman sat next to me. She asked if I'd visited Britain. I replied that I had a B.A. from Cambridge and had lived five years in Britain. "Cambridge does not give a B.A. degree, only the M.A.," the woman replied, adding and ostensibly speaking to me but really addressing the other people at the table, "you did not go to Cambridge." "What the hell," I began but stopped as Vicki dug her fingernails into my thigh. "You did not attend Cambridge," the woman repeated, speaking louder.

"Perhaps life is a dream, as songsters often declare," I said to Vicki later. "Maybe I didn't attend Cambridge or, for that matter, Sewanee and Princeton. Maybe I'm not a teacher. Maybe I'm not married. Perhaps I don't exist." Vicki's observations are often peppery while mine are relentlessly mild. I am also studiously polite. I'm practically as courteous as the man who strolled into a hatchery and said, "Don't rise, ma'am" when he walked past a hen sitting on a nest. "Oh, you exist, and we are married," Vicki said. "The woman is a bitch of the first rank." Of course the growl of canis lupus familaris is often a defibrillator banging the inert into breath. People profess that they like the orderly, the beautiful, and the pleasant, Charles Dudley Warner wrote. "We can find them anywhere—the little bits of scenery that please the eye, the pleasant households, the group of delightful people." Why, then, he asked, do people travel? "We want the abnormal, the strong, the ugly, the unusual," he answered rhetorically. "We wish to be startled and stirred up and repelled. And we ought to be more thankful than we are that there are so many desolate and wearisome and fantastic places, and so many tiresome and unattractive people in this lovely world."

For my part, alas, I prefer the company of the genteel and the amenable to that of the abrasive. My son Francis says I am a "gerontophile," that is, I think too highly of the aged. In truth the aged are endlessly entertaining. Photographers take pictures of passengers as they board cruise ships. The first night the pictures are posted in blocks, according to the time people boarded. A typical group, for example, would include photographs taken of passengers who came on board between 1:30 and 3:00 in the afternoon. "You'd think professional photographers would be more imaginative," a man leaning on a cane said to me. "They should arrange the shots according to the ages of the people photographed—65 to 70, 71 to 80, 81 to 90, and then my cohort, 90 and above. That'd be interesting, especially since many of the sweeties who take cruises lie about their ages." For my part I could not find an embarkation picture of myself. I found a shot of Vicki, however. She was bright and smiling. Although I boarded with her, I wasn't in the photograph. A stranger stood beside her, a person I'd never seen before, a grizzled fellow dryer than Death Valley and more wrinkled than the Grand Canyon.

Tony was a typically pleasant "old boy." An eighty-six-year-old widower who had been married sixty-one years and whose wife had died two years earlier, Tony traveled by himself. "But I am not alone," Tony told me. "I carry pictures of Gloria with me. I put the pictures on the table beside my bed, and in the morning before going to breakfast and at night before falling asleep I talk to her for an hour." "Every day tell your wife you love her," Tony said. "You never know when life will change, and if you don't tell her you love her, you'll regret it." I'm more comfortable writing the word *love* than I am saying it. Vicki took

Tony's advice to heart, however. Twice during the next two days she said she loved me, statements that startled and were more affection than I could bear, making me nervous, causing me to wonder if a cardio-vascular tsunami was brewing just beyond the next port. Of course, ambition, not love, is the great disrupter of comfort. Still, moments of discomfort occur even in a purposeless life. As the boat left St. Thomas, I stood on the Promenade Deck and leaned against the railing, watching frigate birds sail the air, one a male, his throat patch scarlet. "Gosh, I've slept well on the cruise," I said to a man standing next to me. "I'm having a fine time," the man replied, "but for years I spent vacations camping in Utah, and at night I dream of camping." "Not me. The ground is too hard and lumpy for my back," I said. "Besides, mattresses in the cabins are awfully comfortable." "They're firm," the man replied, "but I am not comfortable on them. I keep thinking of the three or four hundred other people who have already slept on them."

Not only have the traces linking me to purpose and its yokemate covetousness broken, but my appetites have diminished, especially literal appetite. Filet mignon and rack of lamb, sacher torte and baked Alaska no longer titillate, the latter pair seeming cloyingly sweet, the former meaty soporifics. Rather than the groomed table appointed with linen and silver, I prefer the informal, the grace not mannered into an echo of the Nicene Creed but quick with spontaneity, the invitation to "Pitch In" striking the right gustatory note. Accordingly the dishes that settled into memory smacked of ease, not art or ceremony: in Mexico bananas fried atop a wagon in Playa del Carmen; diminutive pineapples from a stand on the muddy lip of Fig Tree Drive in Antigua; quesitos at Twin City Coffee in St. Croix; and from Utter Delight, a shed above Magens Bay on St. Thomas, Kailua milkshakes. From a cook near the flea market on Fort Street in Belize City, I bought lunch—red beans, rice, potato salad, and pigs' feet. On Conde Street in Santo Domingo Vicki and I sat across the square from the Holy Metropolitan Cathedral, ate roasted chicken, and drank Presidente beer. In front of us tides of pigeons swept across Parque Colon while tourists clustered in flocks then broke, swirling into shopping, buying straw hats, cotton shirts, and beaded necklaces from strolling vendors. On Roatan after snorkeling for an hour off West End, we sat at the only table on Cindy's porch. Behind a railing Cindy fried snapper for us, serving it with beans and rice. On Grand Turk we ate lunch on Front Street outside the Odd Fellows Lodge, now a liquor store, sitting by ourselves at a picnic table, a Caribbean pine at our backs. We bought Turk's Head Island Draught at the "Lodge," munched conch fritters, prepared four for a dollar in a portable fryer next to the building, and marveled at the sunshine, blue sea, and life's gifts. After two beers and six fritters, I grabbed Vicki's right hand and quoted the hokey old rhyme, "By all the snakes that squirm among the bush and brakes, I love you better than buckwheat cakes."

Food rarely makes me queasy, and from sidewalk carts I never carry away unwanted internal souvenirs. On St. Vincent, Vicki and I drank Hairoun lagers and munched platters of rice and beans, chicken drumsticks, salt fish salad, herring atop dumplings, and cooked plantains. From a man on Bay Street we bought slices of fruit cake, both the batter and the moment seasoned by marijuana fumes billowing from beer huts surrounding the bus station across the road. In a stall off the Circus on St. Kitts, I bought a bowl of Goat Water from Bradshaw. Goat Water is soup made from carrots, potatoes, breadfruit as thickener, and goat, more bones than meat. Market women told Vicki the water caused men to experience "the tickles," warning her that if I swilled more than a bowl I'd never leave her alone. Vicki refused to taste Goat Water, but later she sat on a bench on the street outside Bradshaw's stall and ate lentil patties we bought at "Watch No Face," a green and yellow "Rasta Truck" parked along the curb. The patties were spicy, and we knew they'd make our stomachs billow, but they were so tasty that we risked gale force winds and ate a half dozen, tamping down their effects with Carib beer.

Travel magazines gloss their pages with superlatives in hopes of awakening lethargic sybarites and teasing open their wallets. In contrast animals, especially birds, quicken my spirits. "The conversation of men who could not tell a coot from a moorhen is not of a kind to hold out any hope that, when all the birds have been silenced, the bores will have been silenced, too," Robert Lynd declared. Birds awaken curiosity, kicking lift into my steps and conversation, and peeling gray rind from my eyes. For me they are practically nostrums, one of those nineteenth century patent medicines, a bottle of which, quacks claimed, could transform an old man into a young man "with enough left over to make a small dog and scratch a one-ring flea circus onto its back." In the Bahamas a burrowing owl hunted lizards in a ruffle of scrub behind a beach at Half Moon Cay. A cattle egret perched on the haunches of a goat walking the shoulder of a quiet road in Antigua. Flamingoes and black-necked stilts foraged salt pans on Grand Turk; brown boobies diced a hash of rain and sun above a small bay on St. Thomas, and on Curacao a caracara blustered about atop a divi divi tree bending branches. One morning after breakfast I watched masked boobies frolic beside the ship as it sailed past Cuba, the birds soaring into smiles then dipping and falling into frowns, almost tagging their shadows. Bananaquits ticked shrilly through shrubbery at Nelson's Harbor on Antigua late in the afternoon. With a line of white bunting above their eyes and with white and yellow cinched over their chest and bellies, the birds seemed to be wearing gay boat club blazers. Lesser Antillean bullfinches flitted through brush at the edge of a rain forest on Dominica, the red under the chins of males looking like kerchiefs, while deep in the forest a lesser Antillean peewee perched on a twig stripped by insects.

Vicki and I often drifted from the stabilized routine of the ship, hiring drivers to take us to Mayan ruins. We walked by ourselves, and the landscapes seemed runners decorated with crumbling temples and birds winging gauzy across the shutters of sight. At Quiriguá in Guatemala a blue-crowned motmot perched on a limb, its long tail ending a pair of diminutive rackets, their feathery stringing wet and deep blue. At Tulum the breast of a tropical kingbird glowed like butter while a stole of iridescent blue hung royal over the shoulders of Yucatan jays. Chacchoben was almost an aviary: great kiskadees, ovenbirds, yellow-backed orioles, white-winged doves, and clay-colored thrushes. A brown jay hardened on a branch, its neck looking like a blister spreading over bark while red-throated ant tanagers foraged through trees, the reds on their sides rising over their backs becoming brown in the shade.

The person who eschews purpose is free to meander. Generally he is indifferent to hierarchy and order, thinking them convenient fictions, and sometimes, alas, indifferent to the sad doings of humanity. For my part I'd rather look at animals than think about the world's problems. The butterflies on The Butterfly Farm in Aruba were the ordinary, beautiful, enticing butterflies found in conservatories throughout North America: emerald swallowtails with green wing bands, seductive iridescent blue morphos, and zebras, yellow slashes across their wings looking like they had been applied with a writing brush. Flames flickered through the air in orange bursts, and necklaces of red gemstones clung to the hind wings of rose swallowtails. At the farm I saw two butterflies I had not seen before. While malachites puddled on my arms, their green and black smacking of imperial Russia and for a moment making me imagine myself regal, Indian leaf wings settled on twigs and raising their wings became almost unnoticeable, looking like rusty autumn leaves.

At Tulum, iguanas sunned atop shattered ledges resembling medieval gargoyles. In the Belize Zoo king vultures transformed a barren tree into a Mayan frieze. In the background howler monkeys swung barking through the brush. An ocelot paced the perimeter of an enclosure while a jaguar raised its head from the ground and studied me, after which it flicked its tail and let its head drop back down. An aviary in the botanical gardens in Kingstown held several pairs of St. Vincent parrots. The birds were endangered, and keepers hoped they would breed. The birds had not cooperated and barely moved while I studied them. Instead they stared through the wire of their cages, eyes fixed on an indefinite distance, their heads almost engravings, enervated and rainy with pale shades of white, yellow, blue, and green.

Wandering is chancy. The zoo was thirty miles from Belize City. Two taxis broke under us, the radiator of the first spewing a fountain of green and yellow. The second coughed to a stop ten miles from the port after a plastic sack blocked the air intake. Generally our wanderings were arbitrary. As a result we noticed oddities. In Charlotte Amalie in St. Thomas Vicki bought stamps in order to mail postcards to friends. Sketched on the stamps was a polar bear. "Not a creature often seen in these waters," Vicki said. Behind King's Wharf a barbed fence surrounded Fort Christian. "Temporarily Closed for Restoration until Summer 2006," a sign explained. "This is the last day of 2010," Vicki said. "Time is less purpose driven in the Caribbean," I said, "more sensible and more civilized." Certainly we escaped schedule and mastered time off the ship. Our sauntering resembled the note I found on the classroom floor, scraps interesting to us and to others only if seasoned with words. "There is nothing about pancakes," Stella Gibbons wrote in *Cold Comfort Farm*. "It's only the syrup you put on them." Sometimes, however, the syrup was bottled in the United States, homogenized then exported. Parked on the sidewalk beside Calle de San Francisco in the old colonial section of Panama City was a Mercedes. Pasted to the back window of the car was a sticker reading, "Proud Parent of an Honor Roll Student. Oxford International School."

We meandered alone through St. John's in Antigua on a dark, rainy morning. Near the dock stood a wall painted blue, eight pointed gold stars speckling it. Printed on the wall was "Don't Litter and Don't Forget to Pray." Except for *Pray*, the letters were squat and block. *Pray* was in cursive. "Poetry," I said to Vicki. "Put your hand in the hand of the man who stilled the water," the gospel song urges. For the purposeless, particularly for an aged person cruising the sea of life, letting an omnipotent being determine direction is tempting. For a blink of time, we stuffed our hands into our jackets and followed, not the lead of a deity, but the sounds of the faithful singing. For an hour we stood on a sidewalk beside Bishopsgate Street across from the Pilgrim Holiness Church. Occasionally we rested on a bench in front of Snackette. Printed in red and yellow on the slats of the bench was "Excellent Nails & Beauty Salon. Contact Sophia."

"Holy, Holy, Holy," a woman in the church sang repeatedly, her voice dusky and melancholy, at first rising heavily until it soared into lightness and winged hope. Eventually a preacher spoke, his voice seeming to flow through a canyon creating echoes of itself and breaking on granite ridges, before gathering and rolling forward. "Let the presence of God fill this place today," he cried. "We take authority in the name of Jesus," he shouted, endlessly repeating, "In the name of Jesus." "There is gravy in that preaching, giblets and heart, gizzard and desire," I thought, paraphrasing a description of a sermon I'd heard as a child. The rain soaked our clothes. "Let's return to Heritage Quay and swill a couple of Wadadli lagers. They'll dry us out, and we can talk about breeding black canaries to sell at funerals," I eventually said, my words secular and absurd, separating me from the naked, and disturbing, emotion of song.

I'm not pious, but I spent much time in churches, seeking respite from badgering tourism and searching for quiet words hinting at stories. In Christ Church Cathedral in Nassau I studied memorials. "In Memory of Emma Clementia Blatch," an inscription read, "Whom it pleased the Almighty to visit suddenly in the bloom of life with a severe fever of which she died, October 16th, 1825, aged 19. Her earthly remains are deposited in Potters Field.—Her spirit is with God." "Reader! Whoever thou art," the inscription urged, "Let the sight of this monument imprint on thy mind, that young and old without distinction leave this world; therefore fail not to secure the next." Carved above the inscription, a body wrapped in a shroud lay on a coffin. A woman knelt weeping beside the bier, her head and right hand resting on the corpse. In St. John's Parish Church in Barbados, the epitaph of Ann Isabella Sealy, who died at forty-eight in 1859, declared, "The last privilege vouchsafed to her on earth was that of teaching her husband and children how a Christian ought to die." Not all church writings were so conventionally instructive. A poster attached to the door of the "Church of Signs and Wonders Ministries, Inc." in Frederiksted, St. Croix, advertised a Prophetic School, this under the tutelage of the resident "Master Prophet" whose inspiration arose, the advertisement implied, from his collection of degrees, among others, a "PhD, DD, and THD."

In Cockburn Town on Grand Turk, we wandered into Her Majesty's Prison built in the nineteenth century to house runaway slaves. The prison shut in the 1990s and was a tourist site until a hurricane shattered it in 2008. A door in the wall of the prison tilted open, and we slipped inside. The courtyard had become a tip of plastic garbage bags, lumber, roofing, and crushed stones. Sprawled amid the bags lay nineteen Teddy Bears, their legs and arms contorted, their hair matted and shining almost like fish scales. The bears had been intended for sale as souvenirs. Each wore a short-sleeve, black and white shirt. On the chest of the shirt was a medallion—in the middle shined a gold crown. Printed around the edges of the medallion was "Her Majesty's Prison." On the back of the shirt was "I Can't Bear To Be Without You." "Jesus," Vicki said, "This is horrible. The bears look like children, the sort of terrible sight one sees on the news damn near every night. What do you make of it?" "I don't want to make anything out of it," I said. We left the prison and walked across Pond Street. A heron stood on grass bordering a salt pan. "Is that a tri-colored heron?" I asked. "No, a great blue," Vicki said. "An aimless joy is a pure joy," I said, looking at the bird and remembering a line from Yeats's "Tom O'Roughley." "Yes," Vicki added, emending the poem, "And happiness is a heron, not a gloomy bird of prey."

Time Out

I have run up and down pages for thirty years. I'm tired and am having trouble rebounding from one essay to another. I am calling "Time Out." I plan to loll on the bench for a while. Before I return to tossing verbs around, I'll eat a hot dog, a fat kielbasa covered with dollops of ketchup and mustard and, oh, yes, on top fried onions woolly and thick as a sweater. Afterward I'll study the playbook. Maybe I'll learn a new trick, and the next time I open my tablet, perhaps I'll forsake the dependable set shot and try to pencil my way through an alley-oop. On the other hand I might abandon the game, creep off to the locker room, and in the quiet under the court scrub letters out of my hide. "After a man has passed the psalmist's dead line of seventy years," John Burroughs wrote, "he becomes more and more detached from the noise and turmoil of the times in which he lives." Before bed every night I read the aging man's lullabies, adventure novels, the heroes of which are cleaners, people who neaten society dispensing justice but paying no attention to the law—Thomas Perry's Butcher Boy, Lee Child's Jack Reacher, and James Lee Burke's Dave Robicheaux and Clete Purcell. After a dozen unspeakable villains have been culled and pulped, I fall into a calm sleep.

Once I am out of the game and on the bench I intend to ignore the huzzahs celebrating all the new academic ways. Last month I was appointed to a hiring committee in the English Department. Before the dean allowed the committee to convene, we were required to attend a presentation on "gender equity." The presenters exhibited a chart depicting departments in which the number of male faculty members greatly outnumbered the number of female. "Do you understand that you are addressing a committee of the English Department?" I interrupted. When the presenters looked puzzled, I continued. "Do you realize that the number of women faculty members in this department is 36 and the number of men 31? Do you know that the last four retirements have been males and that this year two more males will probably retire? Lastly do you know that we have been told we can interview eight people for two positions, so long as most of them are women?" The presenters admitted they knew little about the English Department except "its name." "All right," I said, after conversation dribbled along in a desultory fashion for a few minutes more, "the time has come to end this meeting." "You have been helpful and astonishingly informative," I continued, standing and addressing the presenters, "thank you." Of course the meeting did not end so smoothly. That night despite the happily homicidal antics of the Butcher Boy, I slept fitfully, in the early morning dreaming that dusk transformed English from an academic department into a maternity ward. Contributing to my unrest was an e-mail I received at ten-thirty that evening. That morning in my class I handed out an assignment sheet on the short story. Printed on the sheet were the stories to be read, the dates on which they should be read, and the textbook in which they were found. "I am so confused," a student wrote. "I can't find tomorrow's story in the book." "Open your book to the Table of Contents," I wrote. "The Table is in the front of the book. Read it. The third title listed is the story assigned for tomorrow. Beside the title of the story appears the number of the page on which the story begins. Turn the pages of the book until you find that particular number. Once you discover the beginning of the story, start reading."

A fortnight later, I received another e-mail. "I haven't attended the first weeks of class," a girl wrote. "What did I miss?" I had no idea what the girl missed. The girl's wattage was low, and when she eventually appeared, she flickered on and off. What she'd have pondered in the classroom would have had little to do with the course. One morning after a discussion of Sherwood Anderson's story "Hands," she raised her hand and asked if I liked rum raisin ice cream. "That's my boyfriend's favorite," she said. "My favorite is peanut butter swirl." The boyfriend was the girl's only subject. "When he takes off his shirt, he's so cute," she volunteered one morning. "The hair above his pinkies is curly and looks like eyelashes. When he flexes his muscles, his chest winks at me. Isn't that so darling?" If the Angel Gabriel appeared dressed in gold chaps and swooped about the room singing "You Are My Sunshine," the girl would have ignored him unless, of course, he resembled her boyfriend. Certainly she would not have thought about what I mulled when the class dragged: Van Wyck Brooks's quip that "earnest people are often people who habitually look on the serious side of things that have no serious side" or Will Rogers's statement that after William Wrigley realized that "the American jaw must wag" he invented chewing gum as "a kind of Shock Absorber." In the middle of a desultory discussion of "Bartleby, the Scrivener," I sauntered out of Melville's dead letter office and wandered onto a farm. The owner was plowing with a yoke of bulls. "Why aren't you driving your tractor or using the pair of Percherons that are in your barn?" a neighbor asked. "Bulls aren't made for plowing." "I know," the owner replied. "But I'm an educator. I have my animals' best interest at heart, and I don't want these bulls to get accustomed to thinking life is all romance."

During the time out I thought about what I might write in the future. Near the end of their scribbling careers, essayists often turn out books focusing on single topics. Agnes Repplier, for example, wrote *In Pursuit of Laughter* and Joseph Epstein, *Snobbery* and *Friendship*. *Your Retirement*, I reckoned, suited me hooked up to Social Security, and comfortable on the sidelines, shoe laces dangling, a warm-up jacket tossed over my shoulders. I considered beginning a chapter on politics with H. L. Mencken's assertion that America was a nation of evangelists. "Every third American devotes himself to improving and uplifting his fellow-citizens," Mencken wrote, adding, "The messianic delusion is our national disease." Although theological doings are more often than not indistinguishable from politics, religion deserved a separate chapter. Because many of the people who read *Your Retirement* would be grandparents, I thought tips on how to talk to grandchildren would be useful. When angelic Melanie asked Memaw if Jesus was a Catholic, Memaw could answer, "No, sugar toes, He won't a Catholic, but don't you worry none. He ain't going to Hell. He was good enough to be a Catholic." When weensy Tittle Tommy became bored, Boompa could suggest the religious equivalent of "Snakes and Ladders," racing to read the whole Bible in six days. If they succeeded, on the seventh day, Boompa should, I suggested, take Tommy to a sweet shop and buy him a big cone of raspberry ripple ice cream.

In hopes of delaying dementia, octogenarians purchase word games. As a substitute for Scrabble, I suggested samples of the therapeutic games Vicki and I play. At night and early in the morning we chat reversing the spelling and pronunciation of words. "Bed time" becomes "emit deb"; "pardon", "nodrap," and "time to get up", "pu teg ot emit," although sometimes if one of us is slow to come downstairs to breakfast the other yells, "enihs dna esir." Digital clocks have transformed telling time into "medicinal numerology," at least in my house. When numbers such as 2:22 and 12:34 appear, one of us says "attention, attention," after which he repeats the numbers several times. The word *attention* must be said in a deep, toneless military fashion, causing the receptors on faltering synapses to snap together and salute. The hours themselves offer many intellectual possibilities;

thus, for example, the speaker could say 12:21 then follow the initial pronouncement with "backward, 12:21," "inside out, 21:12," "inside out left only, 21:21," and inside out right only, 12:12." The combinations are challenging, and in the early morning hours will invigorate players, preventing them from falling into deep permanent sleeps.

I did not include chapters on the price of gasoline or on intimate doings. Both are inflammatory and messy. For the sake of their wellbeing, the aged should avoid most licenses, the permit that allows them to drive automobiles but especially that other license that gives them leave to misbehave. Although I realized that some widows and widowers among my readers might consider pooling incomes, I wrote nothing about matrimony among the aged, thinking that if relics got together they would, as the old expression puts it, be repairing, not marrying. "When I think of the number of fascinating men and women, I have never known," Aldous Huxley wrote in *Along the Road*, "I am astonished." I planned that the longest chapter in the book would describe the most fascinating people whom I have not known. Neither choosing strangers nor deciding what to reveal about their private lives came easily. In any case I was sidetracked before making my selections.

In the university bookstore, I stumbled across *The Mourner's Bedside Companion*, a volume that intrigued me and pushed *Your Retirement* out of mind. Chapters in the book were split between the poetic and the utilitarian. Among the latter were discussions of wills, estate taxes, insurance, and distant relatives. A lengthy self-help chapter described the best method of haggling over prices charged for coffins and for embalming or cremation. "Do not be satisfied with anything less than a 35% markdown," the author wrote, declaring, "You are not dead. You are alive. The money you save will be enough to paint the house or send you to Florida." The poetic portions of the book focused on matters such as writing obituaries and letters of condolence. A small section provided hints for greeting former acquaintances. "Sight of a corpse thrills and reassures. People whom you have not seen in decades will appear at the funeral home if there is a viewing. You will not remember them. If they take umbrage, hug them and exclaim, 'My god, you have changed so little I didn't recognize you!'" When I told my friend Josh about the *Companion*, he showed me an unpublished obituary he wrote for the late dean of a college in Rhode Island. The dean was short and aggressive. Josh did not like him. Whenever he met the dean, he addressed him as Skyscraper. The dean was notoriously fond of chocolate, so much so that rumor said he overruled a negative tenure decision made by the biology department because the candidate was a marvelous baker, noted for her cream-cheese chocolate cupcakes. "The Dean was a brute addicted to chocolate and....," Josh wrote. "Every Saturday night his wife Clarice baked a platter of chocolate chip cookies for him. These, she said, 'occupied him for the rest of the week and allowed me to go about my business unpawed.'"

I worry that if I stop writing my curiosity will atrophy and I'll miss observing the last minutes of the only game in which I'm the star. The idea that lay at the back of Lewis Carroll's nonsense, G. K. Chesterton wrote, was "the idea of *escape*, of escape into a world where things are not fixed horribly in an eternal appropriateness, where apples grow on pear-trees, and any old man you meet may have three legs." If I snap my pencil, I fear deadening appropriateness will so blinker me that I'll never meet a three-legged man. In *English Humourists*, William Thackeray praised "our gay and kind-hearted week-day preachers." Writers of nonsense soften the fixities of life and make the improbable seem probable. Their books are kindly, and for a moment readers awaken and become converts capable of faith and of accepting the impossible. If I abandon the page, gaiety may vanish from my days, and I may become a dark and censorious realist.

The pen is a liver regulator, and internists prescribe it for virulent cases of spleen and melancholy. Not long ago I read a comment Augustine Birrell made about literature. His words are accurate if one emends them, substituting "Writing" for "Literature." His statement then reads, "Writing exists to please,—to lighten the burden of men's lives; to make them for a short while forget their sorrows and their sins, their silenced hearths, their disappointed hopes, their grim futures." In Acts, the Lord caused a mist and a darkness to fall upon Elymas the sorcerer after which Elymas "went about seeking someone to lead him by the hand." No matter how thick the mist, writers are unable to hide, especially those who teach. Students reach into the dark and grab the teacher's hand then ask for letters of recommendation. Shortly after my time out began, Maureen wrote me. "I need a recommendation for an internship," she began. "I'm a good student, and my interests and accomplishments are varied. At the moment I teach pole dancing and Sunday school." "That is the damndest combination," Vicki said when I read her Maureen's letter. "Put that in an essay. People will believe you because nobody could make that up." "But," I said, "I'm taking time out from writing." "Don't be silly," Vicki said, "pole dancing and Sunday school—wonderful!"

According to an old story, a man walked into a department store. He looked woe-be-gone, bent and whey-faced. A salesgirl saw him and rushed over, saying, "Can I help you?" "No one can help me," the man answered dolefully, "I teach English and sometimes try to write a book." Readers ignore time outs and pat scribblers on the back, massaging them out of lethargy. Almost before I sat on the bench, I received a letter. The letter contained two short poems. "The poems will appeal to you," my correspondent said. "I look forward to seeing them in your next essay." Entitled "The Old Man," the first poem stated, "It was a cold and wintry night, / A man stood in the street, / His aged eyes were full of tears, / His boots were full of feet." "The Careful Penman," the second poem was also succinct: "A Persian penman named Aziz, / Remarked, 'I think I know my biz. / For when I write my name as is, / It is Aziz as is Aziz.'"

After reading the poems, I ended my time out. That afternoon I explored the stacks in the basement of the university library. On its side at the end of a shelf lay *How To Tell Birds from the Flowers A Manual of Flornithology* by Robert Wood. Published in 1907, the book had never been opened. The contents consisted of short poems in which plants and birds were paired, Pea and Peewee, Clover and Plover, being examples. My favorite poem linked Cat-Bird to Cat-Nip: "The Cat-Bird's call resembles that, / Emitted by the Pussy Cat, / While Cat-Nip, growing by the wall, / Is never known to caterwaul: / Its odor though attracts the Kits, / And throws them in Catniption fits." In contrast to their domestic cousins, feral literary cats are not solitaries. Enclosed in a letter I received the next day was a cat story, a version of which I had read a decade ago. One evening a preacher went for a late night walk. He got lost and was forced to sleep in an abandoned house rumored to be haunted by the ghost of a demonic cat. The preacher did not believe in ghosts, and when a small tabby strolled across the front stoop of the house meowing, the preacher laughed and said aloud, "Ghost, my ass. That won't much ghost." "It sure wasn't," a deep voice behind him said, adding, "I guess there ain't going be but two of us here tonight." The preacher spun around. Leaning against the wall was a black cat five feet tall with eyes that glowed like coals. "Uh, huh, and soon there ain't going to be but one," the preacher said, leaping out the door. The preacher ran until he collapsed at the foot of a massive tree deep in the forest. As he gasped trying to catch his breath, the cat sidled up and said, "We certainly had a good race." "Yeah," the preacher said jumping to his feet, "and we're damn sure going to have another one, right now."

I was born with a talent for inaccuracy. It bothered me so much that for a long time I neglected it. "For heaven's sakes," my friend Josh said, "Do you read the Bible? Don't bury your talents. Exhume them. Cultivate them. Water them and spread manure around their roots. Only people blessed with a talent like yours discover the truth about anything." Josh then quoted *Virginibus Puerisque* by Robert Louis Stevenson. "The truth," Stevenson wrote, "is not to state the true facts, but to convey a true impression; truth in spirit, not truth to letter, is the true veracity." The winter of my discontent vanished. I was back in the game. Someday, I thought, I will meet the three-legged man, and even if I don't, I'll tell folks I met him. That will be a kind of truth. People will smile, and life will seem better for them, and me. He is probably the same man who ate the toad and whose wild cattle roamed Mount Sodom. Within a day of Lot's wife's being turned into a salt lick, they'd reduced her to two small crystals. I suspect "Tripod," as his friends call him, plays the fiddle and knows dandy old tunes like "Rattlesnake Shake," "Sugar in the Coffee," and "Sourwood Mountain." He may be the man who owned a pack of chicken-footed dogs that roosted in trees and ambushed opossums. Acquaintances say that the only epitaph he wants engraved on his tombstone is, "Once upon a long while ago he came from Nashville." Someone told me that he tried but failed to breed tuna fish with mermaids in hopes of producing albacore with teats. According to ichthyologists, breast-fed fry grow faster, bigger, and resist blood flukes better than "weaners" fed on squid and crustaceans. He reckoned that because his fish would mature into enormous adults the price of "Bumble Bee" would drop, making it readily affordable for school cafeterias. As a result the diets of students would change. They would eat healthy tuna sandwiches for lunch, and obesity would vanish from secondary schools. Contrary to the *Oxford Encyclopedia of Vehicular Movement*, the three-legged man did not invent the silent bicycle bell. A man suffering from presbycusis created the bell. For my part I'd really like to talk to him because I heard he once found a caterpillar on a pork chop he ordered in a restaurant in Little Rock. I want to know the species of caterpillar. I hope it was something colorful like a monarch wrapped in white, yellow, and black, or maybe a grey furcula whipping its anal prologs about like an officious waiter grinding pepper. I hope it wasn't a dull nubbin of lettuce like a green clover worm or a pudgy corn earworm.

 I must add that although I am eager to meet the man with three legs, other things are also on my mind. Last month I dreamed that the grass in my yard was thick and tall, tumbling over in permanent waves when it reached my knees. Amid the grass lived hundreds of baby rabbits, pudgy Beatrix Potter kits with eyes that shined like polished brown marbles. Late one afternoon while I sat on the front stoop watching rabbits scamper and frolic, thinking they were "adorable," a word I never use when I am awake, a massive yellow school bus stopped at the end of the driveway. The doors whooshed open discharging a school district of Chinese. The Chinese swept across the yard, grabbing and eating the baby rabbits, swallowing them like won tons. When the Chinese got back on the bus, my yard had been pounded flatter than a crew cut and all the bunnies were gone. The dream upset me, and I woke up, wishing that someone—a god or anybody, I wasn't particular—could tell me what it meant. So far no one has been able to help me. "Whatever the dream means, you aren't a racist," my friend Josh said. "There are no rabbits in China, only hares." "That's reassuring," I said then asked, changing the subject to a clearer daylight matter, "Have you seen the exhibition of 'Found Sculpture' at the university art museum?" "No," Josh said, "but what I'd like to see is an exhibition of Lost Sculpture. Not only would it be easy on the eyes, but setting it up would be simple and wouldn't cost much." Oh, well, recently I read an article in *Atlanta Constitution* describing a sect of lizard handlers. Episcopalians can be divided into High and Low Church, the higher the church the lower the sophistication of the congregation. Lizards are snakes with legs. I want to know if lizard handlers evolved from snake handlers or snake handlers from lizard handlers. I'm curious about which group is culturally, and economically, superior. Would a lizard handler permit his daughter to marry the son of a snake handler? I suspect not. Even in this loose, democratic age, some things are just not done.

Walking

This summer I spent six weeks during June and July in Tennessee teaching in the Sewanee School of Letters. Sewanee's campus, or The Domain as it is known, consists of 13,000 acres perched on the western edge of the Cumberland Plateau, most of the land 1900 feet above sea level, 900 feet above the Highland Rim. Atop the plateau is a layer of sandstone. Under the sandstone are conglomerates and thin shale then several hundred feet of limestone. Water percolates through the sandstone and dissolving the limestone digs channels which eventually turn into caves. Almost fifty miles of trails and fire lanes cut across The Domain. The best known trail is the Perimeter Trail, fifteen miles of which follow the bluff on what I call the Nashville side of The Domain.

After Thoreau's death in 1862 the *Atlantic Monthly* published his essay "Walking." Before leaving Connecticut I read the essay, and I decided to spend much of my time at Sewanee walking The Domain. Thoreau's cast of mind differed greatly from my own. He had worked on "Walking" for a decade, and when he died he was only 45. He was young enough to imagine a better world. Metaphorically he urged readers to turn their backs on the east and old, traditional ways of doing and walking toward the west imagine and embrace newness. At 68, I had aged beyond optimism and pessimism and was incapable of fervor, the source of Thoreau's quirky intensity and hectoring didacticism. Moreover Thoreau said that he thought he could not maintain his health and good spirits unless he spent at least four hours a day sauntering through woods and over hills and fields. During my six weeks I spent more than a hundred hours roaming The Domain, fifty-two walking and the rest slowly jogging fire lanes. Only twice, however, was I out for more than four hours, and on both occasions exhaustion so lanced my spirits that they sank rather than rose. Almost always the temperature was over 95 and the humidity over 90%. Moreover in order to insulate myself against ticks, I wrapped myself in long-sleeved sweat shirts and in sweat pants, stuffing the legs of the pants down beneath the tops of thick socks. The trails were often rough with roots and sharp stones, and to keep from breaking an ankle I wore heavy high-topped boots. To protect against sunburn I wore a floppy hat pulled down tightly over my forehead. Lastly in order to see The Domain, I carried the tools of looking, binoculars and hand lenses, notebooks and pens, a knife, and sometimes field guides. These I crammed into the pockets of an orange workman's vest. Within ten minutes of starting to walk, I became fleshly limestone, water soaking my clothes and running off me in rivulets. My underpants became drenched, and some days the cloth bunched together in eroding waves and rubbed the inside of my legs raw.

On arriving at Sewanee, I tried to pare routine and the trivial from my days. I gave up alcohol and stopped reading mysteries and bestsellers. I refused to watch television and glance at newspapers. I didn't answer e-mail, and I decided that I would never again vote in an election. I hoped that loosening a handful of daily life's Lilliputian tethers would so free my mind that once I was in the woods thought would suddenly billow. Of course, nothing of the sort occurred. In an unfenced landscape, a person saunters into doziness, not into inspiration. Confinement is imagination's best catalyst, be its rails Thoreau's Concord or simply the easy habits of a long life. Amid crowds and the barbed rowels of society, blood pressure pounds; irritation swells into thought, and one dreams of escape, shaping stories and fashioning different world orders. In *The Money Box* (1925), Robert Lynd, the English essayist, mulled the push and pull between the hankering for fenceless liberty and the comfort of, indeed desire for, restriction. "Poets seek the confinement of meter and form. Religious men shackle themselves with a creed. Moralists lock themselves in with the iron key of principle. Politicians are unhappy till they have made themselves slaves to a party. It is one of the chief aims of life," Lynd wrote, "to escape from compulsory imprisonment and then, as soon as possible, to submit ourselves to voluntary imprisonment. We must assume the chains ourselves, or Nature will rivet them on us in spite of ourselves."

At Sewanee walking itself became a chain, a green one, hours riveting tangles of ivy, Virginia creeper and grape vine, cat brier, and oriental bittersweet around me. Not until I started roaming did I realize how significance had tired me. In the woods the current of life slowed. Meaning ebbed, and small sights flowed pebbly around my steps, eventually gathering into bars on which I could lounge and appreciate. Thoreau celebrated wildness, declaring "the most alive is the wildest." He got things wrong. The most alive is the tamed, that is, the person so apart from fret that he is calm enough to ruminate. Such a person rarely makes a good neighbor or citizen. He's a poor friend. He is not his brother's keeper. Instead he is the keeper of sunsets and sunrises, fiery searchers, elderberry and cross vine. He uses words not to accomplish but to avoid accomplishment, to distance himself from community and to keep the momentary from swirling about him like a dust devil. He doesn't question because questions often lead to wearying, disruptive action. Instead of charitable, he is self-centered, the high, happy caterwauling of pileated woodpeckers driving the sad melody of humanity from his mind.

In the woods my life belonged to me, not to family or people I met or liked. My blood pressure fell so low that later when I mentioned it to an acquaintance, he exclaimed, "Good

Lord, you were dead." "Dead to many things," I thought, "but not to others." At Sewanee I lived in a guest house on the edge of the Perimeter Trail above Running Knob Hollow and Roark's Cove. Harvestmen crinkled across the ground, the numbers immense. Just before dusk when green still shimmered through the grass lightning bugs pounced into sight as if they had been dusted over a stencil. Cicadas then began singing, and red bats swirled over the spires of Convocation Hall and All Saints Chapel. When I was a boy on my grandfather's farm, I lay on the ground and listened for cicadas raking their way up through the dirt. I caught them and after placing them on logs in my room watched them emerge silver and green from their shells. Once their wings unfolded and hardened, I took them outside and freed them into the air. Cicadas are dear to me, perhaps because I associate them with happy childhood, perhaps because their small barrel shapes make me smile, their eyes poking out to the sides like the business ends of ratchet-handled wrenches. In Sewanee I plucked cicadas from roads. I placed them on the trunks of trees, always checking to make sure that the furrows creasing the bark were not runways for ants. This summer's cicadas were fat, and when cars ran over them, they burst into round blotches purple as plums. After dark, katydids zithered, the sound swelling like leaves opening on trees in the spring and eventually settling into a high coppery rhythm. During a heavy rain I watched a katydid brace itself atop a big grape leaf, its legs struts. The grape wound through a tulip tree. Leaves on the tulip tree were smoother than those of the grape. Moreover silver tinted the burnished veins coursing through leaves on the tulip tree while the veins on the grape were a greenish yellow, the same color as the legs of the katydid.

 The flesh and most of the devil's glittering temptations haven't lured me from the straight and narrow shattering plan and schedule. But the world, particularly the insect world, has long broken both my stride and intention and, turning flesh weak, has dropped me to the earth, at Sewanee the better to observe millipedes, some so armored they resembled art deco streamliners chuffing across the ground, legs rolling like wheels, others with yellow legs skittering. Above their legs the bodies of these last resembled chain mail embossed in yellow. Near the Equestrian Center, I watched a dung beetle tumble a ball of manure across a dirt road, controlling direction with its hind legs, its head away from the ball and toward the ground, the insect's front legs doing the heavy pushing. Grasping the side of the ball was a second dung beetle, stabilizing the roll and looking like a bottle stopper. I roamed the woods at a human not an automotive pace, low hurdles of insects breaking my stride: robber flies, bumblebee mimics, and spider and thread-waisted wasps always in a scurry. In the open end of a damp log crane flies pronged dancing into the air. An orange eczema of vinegar flies spread across a rotten mushroom while a pigmy grasshopper shaped like a tiny tureen sank gray and out of sight atop a dry leaf.

Box turtles inched along sandy upland paths. I picked up all the box turtles I saw. The flat bottoms of their shells sat comfortably in the palm of my hand, and the orange designs across the tops seemed dream-catchers. Not once in 40 years of prowling New England have I seen a box turtle. The poetry of the earth led Thoreau to hanker for a future vibrant with wildness. In the tranquility of The Domain, I imagined a past tamed by sentiment, years when I explored in short pants, the sight of a box turtle great treasure, child's gold of dinner talk beginning, "Guess what I saw today?"

Snapping turtles lurked in water spilling from the lips of culverts behind Sewanee's academic buildings. Although I liked creeping up on them, seeing them did not give me the same pleasure as did stumbling across box turtles. Plotting an approach to the culverts stripped surprise away. Moreover when the turtles noticed me, they vanished, a cloud of mud swirling behind them as they retreated into the culverts. Unlike box turtles snappers seemed almost modern, moving rapidly, not giving memory time to bathe in forgotten ponds or rivers, the mud behind them exhaust fumes.

In yards and at the domesticated edges of woods, animals were familiar and suburban, gray squirrels, rabbits, and the occasional groundhog. Some 22 varieties of snakes are found on The Domain. Snake tales were commonplace, people describing canebrake rattlers big enough to coil treads around Big Foot transforming him into Bibendum, the Michelin tire man. Copperheads turned entrance halls festive, festooning chandeliers and wrapping banisters in gay brown and red ribbons. Because I roamed mid-summer before August dryness set in and snakes began to prowl and because I wandered during the heat of day and did not overturn slabs or rock and wood as I do in fangless Connecticut, I did not see a single live snake. In contrast I came across dens of dead snakes, in the woods, skeletons, ribs so regular they seemed knitted to spines, and on roads snakes flattened into beaded belts, the sort stitched by Plains Indians, copperheads with their hourglass cross bands making the most attractive belts.

The internal combustion motor is a devourer. One morning on the shoulder of highway 41A crossing the edge of The Domain I discovered a bobcat crushed by a tractor trailer, the first bobcat I had seen outside a zoo. The carcass made me forlorn. Much as I knew that ruminating and walking would not insulate me from the "man-traps" of contemporary life, so the bobcat's reclusiveness could not protect him from an industrial death. Aside from packs of feral dogs that roamed the Cumberland Plateau ripping apart tottery fawns, large predators like bobcats had almost disappeared from The Domain. As a result deer were common, tamed both in behavior and to the eye. In yards I could approach within fifteen feet of them before they bolted, the only sign of nervousness the wagging of tails, the black stripe down the middle twitching. Perhaps beauty and elegance initially lure a person from the parlor into the outdoors. Appreciation of variety comes later. Despite realizing that deer had multiplied into cropping destroyers, sight of them made me pause, their slender legs and the golden tan of their coats making me gasp. The woods changed the frames around the deer, and sometimes when I saw a deer, I sat and watched it, once on the slope above Cherry Point Lake below the Forestry Cabin. In the shallows across the lake a deer knelt pulling up and munching the roots of dollar bonnet, a plant that shingled the lake. Above and to my right Queen Anne's lace spread into doilies. Below to the left along the mucky edge of the lake bladderwort bloomed. A red-eyed vireo hurried across the clearing into the woods, its chest white and gray, its russet cap almost scarlet. In the distance a barred owl barked, the sound an echo of itself.

Bored people eat, filling their stomachs when their minds are empty. When the mind is full, appetite diminishes. At the beginning of the School, walking so nourished me that I was rarely hungry. Instead of eating to pass time I ate out of habit and only for strength. For breakfast I drank tea and stirred yoghurt and raisins through granola. For lunch I munched a handful of prunes, slathered peanut butter over a hunk of ciabatta bread, and drank orange juice. Some days I substituted a slab of Mr. Sharp Pasteurized Process Cheddar Cheese for the peanut butter. The cheese was terrible, but it was the best I found at the Piggly Wiggly in Monteagle. For dinner I ate more bread and chose from four main courses: small tins of Beach Cliff Sardines in Water, five-ounce containers of Bumble Bee Chunk Light Tuna that looked like bleached oatmeal, and cans of Bush's

Best Homestyle Baked Beans and Old El Paso Refried Beans, the contents of these two cans lasting three meals after being opened.

My first walks rarely lasted more than two and a half hours. As I ate less, however, I lost weight. As a result I gained energy and walked more. By the last two weeks of school, I'd walked all the major trails and fire lanes on The Domain. Trails I initially hiked from South to North or from East to West, I also hiked from North to South and West to East. Traipsing past familiar spots did not decrease my awareness of Nature's prodigality, but it did lessen spontaneous exuberance, and after an amble I returned to the guest house slightly unsatisfied and hankering for dishes other than beans and sardines. One afternoon late I treated myself to a slice of Key Lime pie in Julia's Fine Foods in downtown Sewanee. The pie was stunningly good, and my culinary anchorite days ended. Julia's sold takeout. On the menu that day was shrimp and grits, a combination so unimaginable to me I purchased a helping. The next day and almost every day until school ended I bought a takeout main course at Julia's, among other dishes, tomato-corn pie; Moroccan chicken, chickpea and apricot tagine; Malaysian inspired tofu curry, and deep dish spinach pie with feta and pine nuts. The night after eating shrimp and grits I dreamed Vicki gave birth to twins, girls named Cheerful and Kindly. "Thoreau didn't have children or ever taste such food," I thought the next morning as I set out to walk from the Equestrian Center down fire lane 14 past Audubon Lake to the Perimeter Trail and on to King's Farm and Armfield Bluff. "He missed a lot."

I got up early my second day in Sewanee and hiked from Green's View through Shakerag Hollow to Piney Point and back, a walk familiar from past trips to Tennessee and one which I repeated five times during the summer. Although the distance was only five and a half miles, hiking was difficult as the trail quickly descended 450 feet down the bluff before climbing back up and stretching out flat and sandy to Piney Point. The day was muggy, the humidity so high and the cover of trees below the bluff so thick that I imagined myself in an aquarium, swimming rather than walking. The canopy waved above me like seaweed while broken trees stretched along the slope looking like the remnants of shipwrecks. Schools of eye gnats swarmed around my face, the watery analogy failing when they slipped into my eyes burning like grains of pepper. The long leaves of walking ferns arched out from their rootstocks amid the limestone and hung outward, the tips searching damp crevices. Bouquets of maidenhair spleenwort spilled from cracks in the bluff, and in sunny spots New York fern spread yellow waving over the ground like seaweed.

    Massive slabs of rock had broken from the bluff and ripped through the underbrush forming reefs of colluvium. The air on The Domain was clean, and lichens bloomed almost as if a Sewanee Appleseed had roamed the plateau casting them abroad in salads: orange sulfur firedot landing on sandstone, on oaks button lichens peppered with black and the rounded green bull's eyes of shaggy fringe lichens, lungwort green but appearing dipped into yellow, shield lichens green and gray, ruffled and sometimes looking like rags, and beside the trail to Piney Point in sandy leafless spots silvery tangles of reindeer lichens. Beside the path through Shakerag whitewash and shield lichens plastered boulders chalky and pale green. Under the elbow bending out from a massive stony box a huge hornets' nest bristled with buzzing. Nearby the Pan pipe nest of a dirt dauber clung to a sharp bare cheek of rock.

    Classrooms are narrow, and in them learning is crafted. Walks are natural. On a walk a person saunters out of the focused, and if he studiously avoids study, amid the mist of experiencing he may amble into appreciation, even belief—

beliefs that exist beyond the distortions of words. I'd rather pledge my allegiance to a great crested flycatcher than to a country. A politician has never brought me to my feet. My pipers of Hamelin are bluebirds, and for years I've followed them through hurdles of low branches and across lawns and pastures. The song of a wood thrush thrills me more than the "Star Spangled Banner." In Shakerag Hollow an orchestra of wood thrushes called unceasingly, their songs not heavy and blanketing but distilled, cooling and invigorating. A worm-eating warbler hopped through dead leaves, and a Louisiana water thrush bobbed along a stream. During the summer I saw mostly yard birds: Phoebes, titmice, sassy brown thrashers, starlings, robins, families of crows, cardinals, hairy woodpeckers, and mockingbirds nonchalantly swooping in long hems. Pileated woodpeckers churred and clacked along the northern edge of Perimeter Trail. Above Armfield Bluff a pair of scarlet tanagers flew into a chestnut oak, the male a red knot tied to green leaves and the papery summer noon. At the western end of the Parallel Trail, blue jays rattled high and shrill through trees while in the dense scrub below towhees frolicked in red and white garden-party vests. Walking teaches that much of life is happenstance. Because most of my walking was under trees, I saw few hawks. One afternoon after returning to the guest house, I muttered, "I wonder if there are any hawks on the Cumberland Plateau." A thwack not a period ended the sentence. A red-shouldered hawk had banged into the study window. The impact stunned the bird, and it dropped to the ground where it lay for two minutes before flying into a nearby tree to groom and recuperate.

 My weeks at Sewanee stretched through the mid-summer furrow quiet between spring's profuse flowering and autumn's milky final gathering. The roots of wild hydrangea pried into creases seaming the bluff overlooking Shakerag, hooking bushes into place as they flared upward in green flames, at the tips of twigs swirls of white flowers. Spiderwort's petals formed a blue cup cradling the blossom's six stamens, these last frothy with yellow. Throws of moss wrinkled atop and along the tilted sides of colluvium. Amid grew the moss patches of spiderwort, small-flowered leafcup sometimes ruffling around them, leaves sticky with tangy fragrance. Stems looking like the ribs of broken umbrellas stuck up from blue cohosh, at their tips round green berries. In the sandy soil along the Piney Ridge Trail bolts of white ran jagged through the leaves of spotted wintergreen. Sassafras and black locust spread shrubby through the understory. Miners had gnawed along the veins of the locust leaves turning middles pale, making the blades look like worn emeralds, the edges green, central facets abraded into dust. Greater tickseed splayed yellow above fans of green, while flowers spun around whorled loosestrife in weak quartets of sunlight.

In residential Sewanee, while day lilies bloomed long-lasting throughout the summer beside drainage ditches and along creek beds, naked ladies sprang up evanescent and pink overnight. Near lakes in the woods on The Domain purple-headed sneezeweed and St. Andrew's cross grew beside trails, the petals of the former drooping lazily, those of the latter small bow ties. Floating hearts carpeted shallow inlets along Lake Cheston. Vines of passionflowers wound through the high grass at the south end of the Farm Pond. Stories say the plant's five petals and five sepals represent the ten apostles, Judas and Peter being excluded, the first because he betrayed Christ, the latter because he denied Him. While the blue and white blossoms have been associated with heaven and purity, the filaments spinning electric around the center of the flower have been compared to the Crown of Thorns. In July wild potato vine seemed to blossom in the dry sand beside every path. Claret gathered at the bottoms of the white flowers looking like the dregs of a rich Communion wine.

I saw flowers I had not seen before: on the Tennessee Williams Trail, tall bellflower, its style a long curved hook; butterfly pea purple lush along the Parallel Trail; and Curtiss' milkwort, candied flowers the size of jelly beans, rosy and dipped in lemon. Studying a flower expanded rather than narrowed vision. Beyond bull thistles growing above a ditch on Brakefield Road, thirty-two horses grazed an endless green pasture, their coats gleaming dun and chestnut, blue roan, gray and bay. Above them cumulus clouds sifted across the sky, the moment making them frolic. While I looked at silver spotted skippers clinging like brown and orange petals to the blossoms of button bush beside Audubon Lake, a catbird mewed and a deer walked out of the woods into the water and like my vision drank deep. In July The Domain was rich with mushrooms blooming into spores: russula, cortinarius, and boletus, among scores of others. At the edge of the plateau just above Shakerag a destroying angel gleamed like waxed snow. Beside the trail golden and red chanterelles gathered in fairy groups. Orange mycena congregated on a log. Both the caps and stems of sulfur cavaliers were yellow. The colors of mushrooms changed like Harlequin's costumes, the cap that was bright and soft one morning tossed aside the next for one blocked and hard. Colors spun in bull's-eyes around a shelf fungus at the base a dead tree, yellow on the outside then pink, orange, blue, and gray. My favorite mushroom was the black trumpet. Small bands stood beside the path to Piney Pine, mouths of the trumpets black and gray, sometimes curving back on themselves in rolls like the sound of taps, the edges wavy.

While I roamed The Domain, banisters of trees steadied my steps. They also steadied my sight. Trees temper ego and pride. Under a big tree one realizes his insignificance, and no matter the pitch of the slope on which he is standing life suddenly stretches out temperate ahead of him. Porticos of large trees grow over The Domain. Colonnades of such trees transformed Shakerag Hollow into a sanctuary. In the broken radiant light the gray bark of tulip trees eroded into brown then flowed into green; here and there twigs jutted out from their trunks, at their tips bright surplices of soft leaves. A yellow buckeye lay fallen across the path looking like a great altar rail, and on a white ash, ridges of bark laced into and through each other, woven inextricably into one like the Trinity. Black walnuts lay on the ground, their husks green and oily, round candles waiting to be broken open into flame. In Shakerag the trunks of shagbark hickory shredded into damp gothic shakes while a thorny crown of sprouts circled the trunk of a huge basswood. Atop the drier northwestern edge of the plateau noonday heated the canopy of chestnut oaks and pignut hickories into simmering, cooking the leaves of the latter into incense. One morning a garden of tiger swallowtails blossomed and flew through and above the canopy, their shadows wavering and mottling the sandy ground. A blackgum curtsied above a slow stream, leaves glistening as if baptized. Three big-leaf magnolias grew up the side of a sharp, open gully, silent string sections of viola-shaped leaves whirling over the trunks. Near Dotson Point the Perimeter Trail wound through chapels of laurel. Off Armfield Bluff grape vines climbed through bell towers of trees, often shellbark hickories, their fruit heavy green clappers.

Although silence flourished amid the trees, I occasionally met people. I began and ended many walks near the Equestrian Center on Brakefield Road. Some mornings at the stable, I ran across Gene, one of my students. Gene had brought his new mule Katie to Sewanee and boarded her in a paddock at the center. Katie was two years old. She was out of a Tennessee Walking Horse and was so beautiful that passersby stopped to admire her. Twice on fire lanes I met mountain bikers. The bikers peddled in quick jerks and did not seem to be enjoying themselves, much less noticing their surroundings. One afternoon Marshall Hawkins picked me up near the beginning of the trail leading to Solomon's Temple, a cave. I had been walking for three hours and welcomed the ride back to the Equestrian Center. "This is the worst year for ticks I've ever seen," the Marshall said. During the walk I'd flicked two lone star ticks off my sweat pants. Lone star ticks transmitted Ehrlichiosis, the most common tick-borne disease of humans in Sewanee. Near Green's View I talked to Mrs. Sholey who told me that she'd trapped a mother skunk and four kits who resided under her porch and who sometimes "quarreled, perfuming the house." Mrs. Sholey turned the skunks loose in a state forest near Tracy City. "They knew I wasn't going to hurt them," she said, "and didn't complain about my putting them into the back of my pickup." Near King's Farm I ran across Mr. Ferris and his black lab Lucy. Mr. Ferris was from Winchester, and he and Lucy were both old and overweight. Mr. Ferris had worked for the state of Tennessee for many years painting bridges. "When I started, I didn't wear any safety equipment," he said, sitting down on a log. "I just held on." "Sort of like we are doing now," Lucy seemed to say, lying at Mr. Ferris's feet and panting heavily.

    On walks I spent more time in the company of the dead than the quick. In Sewanee one is to a graveyard born. Professors and Episcopal dignitaries, and once their servants, and now some alumni are buried in the Community Cemetery. Other folks are buried in the Eastern Star graveyard, two hundred yards and a social class away. As could be expected grass in the Eastern Star graveyard was green and trim, and graves kept well, all stones upright and scrubbed. The Community graveyard was ratty and rocky. More moss than grass covered the ground. Cedar grew scraggily amid spindly red maple and dogwood and the occasional white oak. Stones tilted akimbo, and wrappings of lichens pocked names and erased inscriptions. On the ground at the entrance to the graveyard was a small metal plaque. Printed on it was "Caution Underground Telecommunications" and "Route," arrows on each side of this last word, one pointing into the graveyard, the other in the opposite direction toward Georgia Avenue. The graveyard was familiar with names I knew during my student days, though no one communicated with me by under or above ground means while I puttered about, among others, Rhys, Lancaster, Harrison, Lytle, Chitty, and Gilchrist. Most inscriptions were terse, "I Love You Jesus—Amen" being typical. I did not linger in either graveyard. In the woods life was quicker. Only once did I attempt to resuscitate memories of an undergraduate me. I looked in the window of the room Ed Hatch and I shared in Hoffman Hall in 1961. The room had become a laundry, the sight bleaching recollection.

One morning I left the woods and instead of walking, canoed the Elk River with John Gatta, Dean of the College and an old friend from Connecticut. John and I put in at Old Dam Ford Road and got out at Dickey Bridge fourteen miles later. The river flowed quietly, and we easily avoided snags, paddling past Parks and Dickey islands and around Derrick and Sullenger bends. We set out in a storm. A mop of dark clouds hung over the water dropping rain. Thunder banged like a heavy wooden box knocked shattering off a high table, splitting jagged along the grain into lightning. After the storm thumped away, the day remained cool and overcast. Clouds of mist billowed over the river, at times white, other times soiled and gray, protecting us from sunburn and clarity. Thoreau called Walden Pond the "earth's eye; looking into which the beholder measures the depth of his own nature." For me the mist was the river's eyelid, a shutter that obscured and, freeing me from observation of self, and others, allowed me to drift through moments. In truth many other people were on the river, but they weren't immediately visible. Moreover they traveled in schools, often swirling around themselves then beaching to eat and drink. For John and me, the river was almost silent, and we curled through long stretches without seeing or hearing anyone.

The Elk was another Perimeter Trail, not dipping into coves then climbing and meandering high sandy patches but a trail nevertheless, wrinkling and looping through a green landscape. Massive sycamores leaned over the water then swept upward in mottled brushes to gather sunlight. Glistening bags of ivy hung from their branches. Once the vines reached the water, they turned back and climbed themselves creating pleated bundles of green leaves. Nutlets swung from hophornbeam in pendants. The pendants were so thick that the trees seemed poitrines hung with jewelry. Gelatinous mushrooms gleamed on snags stripped of limbs and reduced to oily logs. On other snags ebony jewelwings gathered in great congregations. The wings of the damselflies jutted up, and in the mist the logs bulged like rocks feathery with polypody. Muskrats swam near banks, and map turtles perched on fallen limbs looking like ridged bottle caps. A great blue heron flapped low around a bend ahead of us, and fourteen buzzards roosted in a dead tree behind a spit of gravel.

John and I had been friends so long that I might have been paddling with a second me. In general life off The Domain was intrusive and overly familiar. In shops I couldn't browse. As soon as I entered, clerks rushed over and asked, "Can I help you" or "How are you doing today?" While the busyness of nature distracts and draws attention away from self, the business of buying and selling refuses to let a person forget himself. In the woods moments were simultaneously bare and bountiful. Along with acquisitive hankerings, I shed the habit of hoping to experience the lightning of sudden truth. The woods were home to butterflies, not epiphanies. And butterflies were good enough. Some days the sky seemed a shoji screen, butterflies brushed across it: red admirals, question marks silvery blue outlining their wings, crescents, pearl azures, and great spangled fritillaries, brown molding out dark and furry from their thoraxes and weeping into orange broken by white ponds. Male red spotted purples puddled the air and ground, their hind wings icy shimmering blue fans cooling moments. Swallowtails patrolled the woods, their flights quick loops: pipevine, tiger, and black. A zebra swallowtail hurried through a dark muddy sink in the woods, flying up and down like a bat, and a spicebush swallowtail caterpillar bundled across a fire lane. The caterpillar was mature, green-ribbed and fat, sides dotted with blue, big black and yellow eyespots staring from its thorax. Underwing moths patched themselves into the bark of trees. They broke loose when I walked near, billowing like thin chips of airborne wood before settling on the far side of other trees. In the Community graveyard haploa moths clung to stones, clymene and Leconte's. The forewings of the first were yellow and trimmed in black, orange at the lower tips. When the forewings were folded together into an arrowhead, the black trimming formed a heavy black sword with thick hand guards above the moth's thorax. Wings on the Leconte's were white and black, with a bump of yellow at the tips. When folded together, the wings formed a design resembling an incense burner, iron and angular as Chinese letters.

 Despite his protestations Thoreau's thoughts focused as often on the distant as on the immediate. Time boils down not only a person's sap but also his capacity for the abstract. What remains is grainy and close to the ground but oftentimes sweet. In the woods dragonflies wrinkled across sight and around the shrubby edges of lakes, their wings shiny as melted sugar.

Sparkling jewelwings bubbled over pools at the mouths of drainage pipes, the stigmas at the tips of the females' wings white motes catching the eye. Prince baskettails flew the low shoreline along Cedar Hollow Lake, their wing beats feeble and slow, abdomens bronze in the light. The hind wings of calico pennants were red with saddlebags while those of widow skimmers were black, white floating weary beyond the bags on males. Stamped on the thoraxes of Cherokee clubtails were chartreuse *M*'s, the legs of the *M*'s curving inward at the bottoms like claws. Yellow ringed the black abdomens of tiger spiketails, and atop cattails eastern pondhawks perched, their abdomens almost petals drying and rolling inward to blue and purple. Whitetails, banded pennants, common baskettails, and blue fronted darners swarmed the lakes on sunny mornings, shedding brightness and sprinkling color through the air, almost stopping Time.

Thoreau ended his "Walking" on a high inspirational note, writing poetically, "So we saunter toward the Holy Land, till one day the sun shall shine more brightly than ever he has done, shall perchance shine into our minds and hearts, and light up our whole lives with a great awakening light, as warm and serene and golden as on a bank side in autumn." When the School of Letters ended, I didn't saunter toward the ineffable. I drove back to Connecticut and family. I had another life to live and other places to roam. Last week near the beaver pond a little green heron flew into a tree and pushing its bill into the air became a shattered branch. A week ago after midnight I watched a small opossum forage across the front stoop. Four days ago a coyote crossed the road in front of the house, and a red-tailed hawk settled into a hickory outside the window of my study, grooming and occasionally rotating its head, peering down into the periwinkle below. Yesterday was my birthday. The day was warm, serene, and golden. Jack and Suzy, my dogs, dipped their

The Splendour Falls

right front paws in ink and signed the card they sent me. Eliza mailed me the complete *Jeeves & Wooster*, my favorite television show. My friend Raymond gave me three of his old neckties, and Vicki made me a very chocolate, chocolate cake.

Goings

"Angus asked his wife for a second piece of toast. She walked across the kitchen and put the bread in the toaster. She didn't look back at the breakfast table until after the toast popped up. When she turned around, Angus was slumped over dead, his head lying on his plate, eggs on his forehead and in his hair," my friend Greg recounted. Greg and Angus roomed together their senior year in college fifty-one years ago. The previous night Angus's daughter Louise had telephoned Greg and described her father's death. "It was nice of her to call," Greg said. "I loved Angus, and I'll miss him, but, the Lord forgive me, I can't stop wondering how his eggs were cooked. Sunny side up just doesn't sound appropriate, perhaps scrambled because death mixes things up." Greg was red in the face and seemed battered. Two nights earlier, he ate dinner with Fred and Carolyn, Fred's wife. For two decades he and Fred taught psychology together in the university. Eleven years ago Fred moved to North Carolina, and he and Carolyn were passing through Storrs on their way to New Hampshire to see their grandchildren. Two summers ago Carolyn began to suffer from dementia. "Throughout dinner," Greg said, "she never stopped drinking wine, at least twelve or fifteen glasses. The glass was always in her hand or at her mouth. The trouble was the glass was empty. I didn't pour a drop of wine into the glass."

"If life is not always poetical," Alice Meynell wrote in 1896, "it is at least metrical." As a person ages into the sere, the meter becomes more pronounced. Goings outstrip comings, and ignoring recurrence becomes impossible. The sane man, G. K. Chesterton wrote, has "tragedy in his heart and comedy in his head." Chesterton's statement does not apply to the aged. Time imposes consistency. Habit hardens into ways of living, and resisting temptation ceases to be unnatural and becomes natural. Like muscles the mind becomes inflexible, and the estrangement of head and heart eventually ends. Instead of wandering distant boards, comedy and tragedy come to resemble each other like a long-married couple, linking arms and sauntering through their final acts together. On the other hand, though, stagecraft inhibits behavior, and perhaps the doings of life should not be compared to the theatrical. Maybe life should be thought an anthology, that is, a gathering of flowers. The bouquets vary from season to season, spring to fall, youth to middle age. The girl weaves a daisy chain. The matron plants beds of iris, and the widow fills a vase with lilies, and in May, if her memory blossoms with happiness, she turns the house into garden decorating rooms with daffodils.

"Our great and glorious masterpiece is to live appropriately," Montaigne wrote. What is appropriate at one time of life is inappropriate at another. As the proverb puts it, "It is good for children to be lambs but bad for adults to be sheep." The goings, the metrical and expected visits to St. Peter, with which age is comfortable and at which it often chuckles, make youth uneasy. Moreover age scoffs at symbols. For the young, symbols spin the tumblers of nouns and verbs unlocking conversation and understanding. The single key that interests the old is the skeleton key. An eight-year-old's climbing an apple tree at dusk clad in scarlet shorts and not wearing a shirt or shoes does not mean that at thirty-five he will succumb to the Adamite heresy, elope with his children's nursery maid, and after settling on a cannibal island become the kingdom's sous-chef responsible for converting missionaries into Brunswick stew.

His reading, Maurice Hewlett stated in *In a Green Shade*, changed as he aged. "I am now more interested in the author than in his book. That must mean I am more interested in life than art." Quite so, and cautionary maxims that once appeared wise now strike me as deadening. If one followed the advice implied in "experience is a good teacher, but its charges are high," spontaneous joy would be snuffed out before a person left the cradle, and his adult years would pass pinched and penurious. My friend Josh thinks true believers should rewrite the Bible. Instead of thin and ascetic, Christ ought to be fat and greasy, shoulders and thighs splotched with dirt, the real blood of living. He should be an insatiable gourmand who so loves the world that he sweeps it all into his arms: trees, flowers, animals, the deep and shallow seas, tears and smiles, laughter and dark cries, and, of course, women, "many, many women." "Women would teach Him humility and make life absurdly happy. They'd break gray moments into meteor showers and the here-and-now would sparkle." The miracles of Josh's Christ are inventions, first a press capable of printing thousands of copies of the Sermon on the Mount in a second, all man's languages present in a single run; next an airplane, a supersonic jet that would make engineers at Boeing turn chartreuse with envy, after the invention of which Christ would fly around the world, tossing bundles of the Sermon on the Mount out the cargo door. "And," Josh concluded, "He'd never be crucified. All great men and gods run away at least three or four times during their lives. By the time the Romans started hunting Him, my Christ would have high-tailed it across the Sea of Galilee and been long gone. He'd run and run and run. He'd never stop and never die, and wherever He fled, water would flow from the dry rocks of men's hearts and save them from themselves."

As one ages doctrinal difference and worldly position become meaningless. In the tomb a person sheds both denomination and wallet. Unfortunately youth is coursed like a hare, society baying "ambition" and "pride," schools barking "success" and "failure," turning days viral with pressure, and like tularemia causing depression, anorexia, and ataxia. "Teddy and I walked through a tunnel of trees," my student Catherine wrote last week. "We walked past vines that erupted from the ground in scrawny tangles. We passed through a sea of ferns. We didn't know where we were going. Suddenly we turned a corner and found ourselves bathed in sunlight. We were in a beautiful, peaceful place, a lost place that allowed us to be twenty-one. I heard Teddy breathe deeply, and I knew he was happy." "Education has a lot of failings," I muttered as I read Catherine's paper. "Along with shaping, schooling misshapes," I continued, not something I thought forty years ago. An old verse came to mind, one that might have appealed to a youthful me lost in a beautiful place with a sunny companion. Of course now that I look at the stanza, it is clear that Pegasus, poetry's winged horse, has lost all his primaries and most of his secondaries and suffers from stringhalt if not wobbler syndrome.

> When we dwell on the lips of the girl we adore,
> What pleasure in nature is missing?
> May his soul be in heaven—he deserves it, I'm sure—
> Who was the first inventor of kissing.

"Every man," E. V. Lucas wrote, "however unobservant or incapable of correlating experiences must learn something during the course of his life. Some little something." In *Dreamthorp*, Alexander Smith celebrated the "suggestiveness of common things." For me, common things quicken life: a poetic kiss, a plate of eggs, an empty wine glass, and good-humored Jesus rollicking with love, a wreath of goldenrod around his forehead, under his arms Sadness and Ugliness, both lovely beyond compare, forever and ever. I don't ache for the wishing cap of Fortunatus—no felt fedora or hipster's beret for me, just a Panama in the summer and a stocking cap in winter. I have aged beyond pondering meaning into being delighted by little somethings. A statement like Robert Benchley's, "You can't eat your cake, and have it, too" bears endless repeating. How nice to know people in Kansas call horned toads "Oklahoma Mermaids" and that according to a pronouncement by a Lutheran theologian "marriage is a harmless amusement." I now doze during conversations about history. No longer do I struggle to understand the grand doings of nations so that I can make an A. I prefer the anecdotal, the mature student's C-. A missionary in India, I heard not long ago, became upset at the inconsistent behavior of his Hindu followers. On Sundays most members of his congregation dedicated themselves to living new lives, among other things giving up alcohol. By Wednesday they were once again swilling fortified nectar. The missionary consulted a Brahmin, hoping to discover the cause of the backsliding. The Brahmin mulled the matter while chewing betel nuts. "It is because," he eventually said, "that the people don't know whether to give up their jug-or-not." A hundred years ago, Holbrook Jackson wrote, "It is only when life is overwrought with the tyranny of doing that we miss the joy of being; and it is only the consciousness of being that makes us capable of any worthy action." "The sunnier the tale," an old proverb states, "the brighter the day," for the self and for others, I should add. "A person can learn more about the workings of Wall Street by reading 'Puss 'n Boots' and observing the antics of the trickster," a professor emeritus of economics told me, "than he can by studying Keynes, supply-side, macro and micro economics, or any of the other dusty statistical heaps."

I don't travel much nowadays. I won't visit the Dominican Republic and stay in the Peninsula House. I won't deplete my savings and pay $1,480 for a two night stay in the Remota Hotel in Patagonia. I will never stretch out in the Kirawira Luxury Tented Camp in Botswana and imagine myself a big game hunter. I won't wander from my room in the Oberoi Udaivillas

The Splendour Falls

in Rajasthan in hopes of seeing a desert fox or the great Indian bustard. Although I have spent days exploring the Cumberland Plateau in Tennessee, named after the victorious English commander at the Battle of Culloden, I won't fly to Scotland and spend a vacation at Culloden House. I will never unpack a bag in Estonia or Lithuania, Bali or Brazil. I won't drink too much wine in the Napa Valley or get swept off Cape Hatteras and out to sea. No, most of my travel now is to Memoryville. The town is not thriving. The intellectual recession has hit hard. Most stores are abandoned, their fronts boarded up, what's left behind hidden under tapestries of cobwebs. The shoulders of Main Street have vanished, sliding into the sink hole of age. Many side streets are dead ends. Mansions have become boarding houses, their inhabitants weary single men and women. Union Station is a pigeon roost. Two trains pass through each day. In the morning "Time's Arrow," in Loren Eiseley's words, heads north, its passengers only glimpses—opportunities squandered and people almost met. In the afternoon, the Arrow rolls south, the passengers shades, their identities worn thin by the rub of years. Farms on the western side of town have run weedy. Tobacco barns have collapsed into grey woodpiles, and rain has sheared pastures into rills. Only God's Field, the graveyard, is tended. Actually the "Field" has grown, its cultivation spreading across a serving dish of small knolls.

On my last trip to Memoryville, the liveliest place in town was the Tabernacle of Love, Slubey Garts's church, where Obed Eells was leading a revival. Slubey first appeared in my books twenty-five years ago, Obed, a dozen years later. I remembered the Tabernacle of Love clearly, and I entered the church wondering if the interior had remained the same. It had. Slubey has always been a Christian entrepreneur, and the only change I noticed reflected the "March of Commerce." Slubey converted the wasted space on the front of the pulpit into a bill board.

Taped to the pulpit on the first night of the revival was a broadside advertising, "Tuttle's Mortuary and Haberdashery." "In stock Comfortable Coffins soft as the Feathers of the Holy Dove," the sign read. "Also a rack of elegant Slumber Robes, guaranteed to Fit and give Satisfaction to the most Particular." On the second night the sign was poetic, advertising Golder's Formal Dress in Lebanon, reading:

> Oh! Come into the garden, Maud,
> And sit beneath the rose,
> And see me prance around the beds,
> Dressed in my Sunday Clothes.

Obed himself appeared unchanged. He had labored too long in Brimstone Alley to be affected by whimsical theological fashion, and his preaching was immediately familiar. "The Lord is here now," he began urging attention. "He may not be here again for thirty years. You best learn to sail with the gospel, so the next time there's a big rain you can be a deck hand on the ark." "Do you follow the Scripture Calendar?" he asked. "And does your mouth water when you smell religion?" At times Obed was mysterious, shivering as if locked in an icebox, rolling his eyeballs back into his head so that only the whites showed, and moaning, "Beware the Widow of the Wood. Beware her long dress and tiny fingers." Patched throughout the sermon were maxims, some conventional like "Never rake with the teeth up," others less so, "If you smell a rat, crush it in the bud." Obed described people he knew, Ashahel Wheeler who, he testified, was "reliable despite never drinking" and Salathaniel Durdam, a cobbler who "just breathed his last but whose sole was always firm and sin-proof." Obed distrusted sophistication. "Education," he claimed, "kills by degrees." "When Gaynelle says, 'au revoir,' I says, 'watermelon, watermelon.'" He thought medicine suspect. "Take your prescriptions to Jesus," he advised. "He is the only Pain Abolitionist certified by Heaven." When his concentration failed, Obed rested by mechanically reciting couplets, a technique he used in my earlier books, "Oh, may my heart go diddle, diddle / Like unto David's sacred fiddle" being typical. Occasionally he poached verse from a tombstone: "Since I so very soon was done for, / I wonder what I was begun for." He quoted the Bible, his citations startling and keeping the congregation alert. "The fifteenth verse from the two-eyed chapter of one-eyed John," he once said, the translation being from the second chapter (II) of the First Epistle General of John (I), the verse beginning, "Love not the world, neither the things that *are* in the world." Obed was a holy entertainer. To illustrate the lesson that man should know his place, he said, "Birds were created to live in the air, fish in the water, and moles in the ground. Put the first in the element of the second, and they will struggle and strangle. Put the second in the element of the third, and they will flounder, gag, and die. And should moles be so bold as to soar above mountain tops like eagles and buzzards, more than likely they'll get dizzy."

    I grew up an Episcopalian, and I am allergic to bouts of preaching, even when delivered by the lute-tongued. Only twice did I visit the Tabernacle of Love. I also worried that Obed might single me out for the Water Cure, that is, immersion in the baptismal tank beside the mourner's bench. I no longer swim well, and I fretted that fungus might thrive in the pools that settled in my inner ear. My hearing isn't good. I am oblivious to high pitched sounds, and an earache might punch holes in the remnants of my eardrums. Additionally a storm roared across Connecticut in late October dropping two feet of snow in some towns and like a mythological lumberjack felling untold forests of trees. Almost nine hundred thousand homes lost electricity. I was needed in Storrs. On my street the power was out for four days. Vicki and I ate by candlelight and later shivered in bed despite basting ourselves with icings of covers. The sheets were cold, and I wore bed socks. After wearing the socks for a while, my feet felt clammy, and I kicked the socks off. Shortly afterward my feet became chilly again. I tried to pluck the socks from the bottom of the bed with my feet, but I don't have prehensile toes. To retrieve the socks, I pulled my legs from under the covers then burrowed toward the bottom of the bed head first like a mole rat thrashing through a tunnel under the Kalahari. Vicki woke, and becoming a prosecuting attorney accused me of robbing her of sleep, using words more appropriate to the murderously felonious than to nocturnal misdemeanors.

In the last few days I have heard little about goings, and for my part I haven't planned a journey. If possible, I'll stay away from Memoryville for a while. A fellow traveler told me that Obed said that Republicans were mean enough to steal the Cross and break it up and sell it for firewood. I don't believe the story; Obed rarely mentions politics. I realize I should not repeat the account, but it's impossible for a writer to behave like a gentleman. Anyway no one I know is snoozing on the cooling board. Of course if someone is playing his last card, and that includes me, I'd be interested. "Speaking broadly," Alexander Smith wrote, "it may be said that it is from some obscure recognition of the fact of death that life draws its final sweetness." Oh, before I forget, I heard a nice little something. After Obed's final sermon, a member of the congregation named his dog Moreover. "Why Moreover?" a friend asked. "Because Moreover is a scripture name," the man answered. "What?" the friend replied looking puzzled. "Moreover is biblical," the man repeated. "Look at Luke, chapter sixteen, verse twenty-one, 'moreover the dogs came and licked his sores.'" Rather curious, don't you think?

Brabblement

A brabblement is a squabble or in operatic terms the overture to a hubbub. Brabblement is archaic and has vanished from conversation as has, indeed, the world I knew as a child. "Heard melodies are sweet, but those unheard are sweeter," John Keats wrote in "Ode on a Grecian Urn." Not only have my surroundings changed, but they have also grown silent, and hearing the unheard has become almost impossible, rendering my thoughts and concerns obsolete. "When we have ceased to want to hear the postman's knock we conclude that we have seen the best of the day, and that the demon of disillusion has us in thrall," A. G. Gardiner stated in *Many Furrows*. "It is to have given up hope that the legendary ship of our childhood will ever come home. It was that admirable vessel that made the future such an agreeable prospect."

Browning's Rabbi Ben Ezra got matters wrong. "The best of life" is not yet to be but has been, at least if not eagerly awaiting the postman's knock is a symptom of disillusion. Only occasionally do I receive mail. Three weeks ago, however, Sally, a former student, wrote me, and I slipped the arthritic embrace of obsolescence, tossing Browning overboard and picking up Tennyson, for a moment recalling the softer embraces of spring, that time when "a fuller crimson comes upon the robin's breast." "I have wasted the past four years on shoes, wine, and men," Sally wrote. "Happiness is more complex." "Maybe," Vicki said when I read the letter to her, "but the gal has made a pretty good start, especially with the shoes." Unlike Sally's letter, almost all my correspondence pinches, blistering bounce from step and thought. Last Saturday I ran the Hartford Half Marathon. On Friday, the day before the race, I received a letter from Ken, a retired doctor in North Carolina. Ken's health has been poor for three years. "I wish you good fortune in the run," he wrote. "While you are doing the half marathon, I hope to be celebrating walking halfway across my bedroom without using a cane." "Keep Vicki in good health," Ken ended. "Be sure that she does not die before you do. It's terrible when a man's wife dies before he does."

Order deadens, turning people into victims of rules established to make living easier and more comfortable. In *At the Sign of the Van*, Michael Monahan wrote, "In the name of the law, every oppression has been upheld, every superstition guaranteed and defended, every injustice sanctioned, every tyranny maintained, and every advance of the race toward light and liberty banned and thwarted." Instead of sauntering through barrens chewing locusts and wild honey, hair blown into tangles by winds black with the voices of temptation, some of which cannot be resisted, the aged walk from the kitchen to the television room, clutching a box of Triscuits and a bowl of onion dip, or if not that, a tray ponderous with carrots, celery, and hummus, and if they are feeling adventuresome, pita bread diced into triangles.

Age is law-abiding, contemplative and accepting, focused more on the past than the future. Memory is a pistol equipped with a silencer. Recollection does not bang, enlivening the present. Instead it drains vitality and quiets even, perhaps especially, recollections of happy childhoods. "I doubt if there is anything in my life," J. B. Priestley recalled, "that I regret more bitterly than I do my frequent failure as a boy to bring delight to my parents by showing how pleased I was." To slip the leash of remembrance and inject the virus of brabblement into my days, I say things that are almost inflammatory. "Any devil can make a good soldier, but it takes a good man to make a pacifier," I said last month, certain that someone in these warmongering times would be irritated. The remark provoked only one response, this from a man who appeared to have slipped beyond narcolepsy into dotage. "Oh," he said, looking at me brightly, "was that a pun? I believe it was a pun. That was a pun." Disappointed and eager for brabblement, I forged ahead recklessly and confessed to a cardinal academic sin, announcing that I was biased and proud of the fact. "Ever since I could read," I said, "I have been prejudiced against Judas."

In hopes of inspiring a little noise if not fray-nological development, I tell stories. One Sunday morning Anna and Anna Knockley, I began in class on Tuesday, were walking along Read Avenue in South Carthage, Tennessee, when they heard church bells ringing in Bluff Creek. The first Anna Knockley was two years older than her sibling. "When my second little darling was born, I took and give her her sister's name spelled backward," Burleese Knockley explained. "I wanted the girls to be close, but I didn't want folks to mix them up, so I was careful about the spelling, paying as much attention to the consonants and vowels as a schoolmarm up to Nashville." "Upon my word, listen to those bells," the older Anna said; "I've never heard them so clearly." "Yes," the younger Anna answered, "they are more distinct. That's because the new road to Bluff Creek opened. The road shortens the distance, don't you know?" When the class remained silent, I dug another story out of the corn crib. A rumor circulated through the firmament when Attila the Hun was dying. Because "The Scourge of God" had invented so many ingenious tortures, the Lord was considering removing Satan as the ruler of Hell and replacing him with Attila. Upon hearing the rumor, the damned leaped off racks and despite lapping flames and thumbscrews composed a petition begging the Lord not to depose Satan. Practically all of Pandemonium signed the petition. Even those who found the footing slippery because they had been drawn and quartered managed to make their way through eternal night and sign their names. "He might not be a perfect devil," Moloch said, "but damnation, he's our devil." When I finished the story, certain it was better to tell tales in the classroom than reign in the administration, Ashley raised her hand. "Mr. Pickering," she said, "who is Attila?" "And," added Patrick, "who is Moloch and where is Pandemonium?"

"Your stories are too tame to foment brabblement," my friend Josh said recently when he came to my office. "You need real noise makers, a tale rancorous with kazoos, a tambourine or two, maybe a megaphone, a half dozen ratchets, and a box of blow-outs, these last with the head either of Winnie-the-Pooh or John Wilkes Booth below the mouthpiece." Josh paused for breath before pushing forward and supplying an example of the sort of story I should tell. The theological knowledge of deacons serving churches in the Christian republics of the United States is often rudimentary. At a revival in Alabama recently a sawdust-trail evangelist quizzed three elders of the church with the highest lightning rods in Coosa County about Easter. Alas, the first elder mistook Easter for Christmas. The second did no better, confusing Easter with Valentine's Day, leaving it up to the third elder to salvage the reputation of the sanctified. "I'm pretty clear on this," the man began confidently. "After Jesus died, he was buried in Ohio or maybe Pennsylvania—in any case, in a limestone cave. After the disciples left they blocked the mouth of the cave with a boulder. On Easter pilgrims visit the cave and roll the rock away, and if Jesus pokes his head out, that means we'll have six more weeks of bad weather."

Josh was born with a toothpick in his mouth, and his tales are too raw for my palate. I am happiest when brewing my own hubbubs. These usually consist of unheard cacophony. Once every four years Hollis Hunnewell's travelling show appears on my pages and visiting Carthage, camps at the fairground. Although the exhibits take Vicki's voice away and make dinners as silent as those at Trappist monasteries, the shows cause commotions in Carthage. Moreover they disrupt humdrumery and make me smile. After Josh left my office, I pondered this fall's show. The lead performers were The Human Tires, Otis and Floyd Pogue, two acrobats "from Paris, France." The Pogue brothers were double-jointed. Their act featured their bending over, tucking their heads into their chests, and after grabbing their ankles, rolling down hills smoother than any of the four-ply tires sold by Firestone. Unfortunately in a previous performance in Lebanon, Otis delayed too long before applying the brakes and crashed into a blackberry patch suffering a deflating puncture. Hollis's other headline performer was a singer The Florida Flamingo, Belle Friskett. Belle wore a voluminous scarlet dress. Attached to back of the dress atop a bustle was a bouquet of ostrich feathers dyed red. Perched on Belle's head was a round red bonnet from the front of which protruded a large yellow and black replica of a flamingo's bill. From the left side of the lower mandible dangled a scarlet cord, a black knob attached to the end. Sometime during every song, Belle pulled the cord down, lowering the mandible and opening the beak, from the mouth of which swarmed an orange cloud of lady bugs. Belle's repertoire was large. All her songs were upbeat, among others, "I've Got the World on a String," "All God's Chillun Got Wings," "You Are My Sunshine," and "Happy Days Are Here Again." During "The Gospel Train," a whistle blew when she sang, "Get on board, little children." The whistle sounded like that of old 576, a 4-8-4 engine from the Nashville, Chattanooga, and St. Louis Railway, lately parked on a siding in Centennial Park in Nashville. During "I've Got a Lovely Bunch of Coconuts," Hollis rolled out a cart heavy with pitchers of scuppernong wine and baskets of cameo apples. "Not," he said, "the bitter apple that poisoned Adam in Paradise, but a sweet fruit, its flavor cultivated by generations of fallen farmers."

Inside a green tent the right hand of The Arkansas Giant lay on a hay rack. The hand was concrete, and its middle finger was missing, having been snapped off when the back axle of the wagon broke, tilting the bed and dumping the hand on the ground. Hollis was an experienced barker, however, and he patched the damage with virtue, saying that "out of politeness and in order not to offend our Pentecostal sisters and brothers" he had amputated the finger. A short fat man sat in the palm of the hand. The man was bald and toothless. "Ninety-five years old and rescued from an assisted care prison in Poultice Hill, Mississippi," a placard added. On the bed of the wagon to the man's left was a wicker basket full of boiled ears of corn; on his right a tray containing fifteen sets of false teeth. The teeth in each set were arranged differently, one pair, for example, missing incisors and molars, another canines and premolars. Three times during the day the man ate a seven course meal of corn, changing teeth for each course. Eating harrowed the kernels, creating patterns on the cobs similar those fashioned by stitching—double herringbone, threaded back, brick and cross, chessboard, whipped fly, and four-legged knot, among shucks of others.

A glass-topped museum case stood next to the wagon. The display that garnered the most interest was a clear paperweight containing matching "His and Her" moles removed from the foreheads of George and Martha Washington. The moles were brown, and each was shaped like the horn and face of an anvil. The face bowed out slightly, and if looked at closely, the moles resembled the thirteen original colonies. "The horn obviously is New England," Hollis stated. A second paperweight held an orange birthmark removed from the neck of a woman who died in South Carolina not long after the Battle of Gettysburg. The birthmark wrapped the woman's neck like a dickey and except for the color looked like a pair of Duroc shoats. "My word, the poor dear," Ada McClarin said when she saw the mark. "How long did she suffer from it?" "Pretty near her whole life," Hollis said. Nearby on a flat table lay The Two Thirsty Swords. Hollis's assistant, Maurice, said that one of the swords was the ax with which Richard Brandon chopped off the head of Charles I of England. The other was an angled blade removed from the guillotine by Charles Sanson the Royal Executioner after the Reign of Terror ended in France. Drop cloths decorated with fleur-de-lys hung around three sides of the table. Maurice stood behind the table on the fourth side. Out of sight under the swords were small springs. Attached to each spring was an electrical cord. The cords ran beneath the table cloth and snaked down the back of the table to an electric starter motor. When Maurice stepped on the starter button, the springs shimmied and the swords quivered. "They are thirsting for blood. Stand back. Don't come close," Maurice warned in a cavernous voice. Before patrons could study the swords carefully, Maurice lifted a jar of blood from the ground and poured the contents over the blades. The swords buckled making a noise that sounded like a belch after which they stopped moving. "Too many fatty red cells—taking naps after lunch," Maurice said. "Shucks," Googoo Hooberry told Hink Ruunt after viewing the swords, "that won't real blood. I dipped my finger in it and tasted it. I reckon it was Cherry Kool-Aid thickened with pectin or some such of a thing."

A menagerie of the animate and inanimate was on sale at the show. A box contained handkerchiefs with sayings sewn onto them. Many sayings were worldly, "The absent are always wrong" and "Lawyers' houses are built upon the heads of fools," while other sayings were moral, "The tears of sinners are the wine of angels" and "Chance can make anybody great, but being wise or good takes work." A few handkerchiefs were black with funereal inscriptions curving over them in white, "She had no fault, save what travelers give the moon, / Her light was bright, but died, alas, too soon." Some handkerchiefs were pink and decorated with poetic posies, "First love Christ that died for thee, / Next to Him love none but me."

A litter of May kittens played on a rug. Countrymen routinely drowned kittens born in May because according to folklore May cats were poor ratters, preferring to catch snakes rather than rodents. "Guaranteed to keep copperheads out of parlors and basements, barns and outhouses," a sign hanging from a rope above the kittens stated. For twenty-five cents a child could buy a Roman helmet made from the hide of an armadillo. "Just like the helmets worn in Hollywood movies, only smaller to fit your sweetie's little head," Hollis said. For kitchen tables or the dashboards of cars, parents worried about the unruly behavior of their offspring could purchase "durable" plaster of Paris figurines depicting Elisha with his arms draped over the shoulders of his buddies, the lady bears who mauled the forty-two children who taunted him because he was bald. So that children would see that respect for the elderly was rewarded, each of the bears was stroking the head of a good child while handing it a lollipop with its other paw.

Also on sale was a pharmacy of the medicinal. Two baking pans contained black snails. "The best snail for getting rid of warts, much better than green or white snails," Hollis testified. Stacked on a shelf were tins of Samuel Pillblister's Smokeless Memory Snuff. A pinch of snuff invigorated the failing memory. The snuff was a finely ground powder and free from tobacco, its main ingredients being hominy, gardenia florets, black-eyed peas, John the Conqueror root, pansy blossoms, and, "most beneficial," a tincture of elephant dung. With the purchase of each tin, Hollis included a "Poetic License" as a bonus. To draw attention, Hollis placed two Alligator Angels beside the stacks of snuff, on the left side a dark angel and on the right a white angel. The angels were winged alligators. Each alligator was stuffed and four feet long. Attached to plates on the back behind the front legs of the good angel were a pair of swan's wings; behind the legs of the bad angel were the wings of a turkey buzzard.

Hollis said the alligators were "freaks of nature" that his brother Horace caught while trapping snapping turtles in a swamp near Monroe, Louisiana. The truth was that Hollis purchased them. Northeast of Gray, Georgia, on US 129, known locally as the Eatonton Highway, before the sulfur spring at Honey Hole and just after the intersection where Ellis Church Road coming from the east crossed the highway headed west and changed denomination becoming Damascus Church Road was "Tommy's Salvage, 45 Acres of Used Animal and Auto Parts." Several sheds contained the universal joints, crankshafts, ignition systems, pistons, and steering arms of animals, in addition to spokes, studs, and cotter pins for coupling parts. Two floors in one shed were devoted solely to upholstery—leather, feathers, fur, and horny scales among others. Four of Tommy's employees spent workdays fabricating fictional beasts for horror movies and carnivals. Snakes were the creature most in demand. Every week workmen skinned two barrels of rattlesnakes and a barrel of water moccasins, rattlesnakes being popular in the Piedmont and Southern Highlands, water moccasins in the Spanish Moss regions of the Deep South. Often the snakes became children's toys, their bodies oiled and flexible as shammy, a windup motor and loose coils inserted into stomachs, keys jutting out of the cloacae. Occasionally big snakes were fitted with new heads constructed from the skulls of opossums. Because opossums had fifty teeth, many of which were sharp as nails, the market for their skulls was great. Opossum farming traditionally thrived in the southwest, the biggest farm in the country and the supplier of Tommy's skulls located near Palestine, Texas, and owned by a former speaker of the Texas House of Representatives.

For farmers Hollis sold "Duck Wheat from the North Pole." Ten years ago, Hollis recounted, a farmer in North Dakota shot a drake that was flying south after spending the summer fattening in the Yukon. The bird's craw was swollen with seeds bigger than those of "Siberian Buckwheat." In spring the farmer planted the seeds. Sixty days later his crop was in. Every acre planted in Duck Wheat, no matter the soil, Hollis said, was guaranteed to produce at least five hundred bushels of grain. Not only that the wheat was a miraculous invigorator. The farmer owned an ancient gray mare that could barely stand until the farmer started feeding her two quarts of Duck Wheat a day. "Within a month the horse was on her feet and doing the work of two railway mules." "And Mrs. Farmer," Hollis said, "was in worse shape. She suffered from frightful dreams, spavins, untimely wind puffs, and the pinkeye. Her liver was torpid, and she was no sort of wife to her husband." Because Duck Wheat had made the old gray mare snort and kick up her heels, the farmer began adding Duck Wheat to his wife's breakfast gruel. "Six months later the wife gave birth to three bouncing boys, each of them born with hair on his chest and weighing more than twelve pounds." As for the farmer himself, he suffered from scald head and for fourteen years had carted around a hernia bigger than a Yellow Horse apple. A month after starting a regimen of Duck Wheat, the farmer's head was as bushy and as sweet-smelling as a persimmon tree while the hernia had shrunk to the size of a "half-eaten strawberry" enabling the farmer to turn his truss into a slingshot "which he used to frighten crows out of his corn field."

The last day of the show Hollis pitched a small tent near the exit at the back of the fairground. "MEN ONLY," a broadside stated. "Don't miss the Fabulous Bonassus. Sight of a Lifetime. But be Careful. The dung of the Bonassus is so hot that it burns the hair off dogs! Admission one dollar. Showing after dusk."

Sketched on the back of the broadside was the Bonassus itself. The Bonassus had the body of a water buffalo, head of a prehistoric goat, eyes of an elephant, warthog tusks, and shaggy legs four times as thick as those of a male lion. "To ensure the safety of patrons," Hollis said he could exhibit the Bonassus only once. Moreover he limited the number of spectators to fifteen, shepherding these into a knot before ushering them into the tent. Once the group was inside, a flap fell down over the entrance, and the tent was as dark as midnight. Immediately Maurice set off a combination stink and smoke bomb. Hollis then switched on a flashlight, the beam revealing a cage blackened by soot, the door off its hinges, standing beside it two hairless dogs. "Great god almighty," Hollis shouted, "the Bonassus have done absconded! Skedaddle! Run home! Bolt your windows and doors! Lock your beagles in the attic and pray! And yes, if your wife has long hair, chain her up there, too, and call a barber immediately!" Hollis's show did not set off a brabblement although the men who raced home to save dogs and wives from the Bonassus eventually realized that they had been sold. The next morning two of them asked me to refund their dollars. I explained that I didn't manage Hollis's money and suggested they talk to him in person. Unfortunately, I added, the show had left Carthage at midnight and by now was "probably halfway to Bowling Green," its next stop.

Moonshine does not make a person quarrelsome or incite a hubbub. It can, however, make him loony, at least for a moment. After waving goodbye to Hollis as he headed north on Highway 25, I thought the show was over and out of mind. I was mistaken. Soon after I laid my pencil down, Vicki and I drove to the biannual book sale at the Mansfield Library. There the circus continued. As I walked in the door, a man approached me. "Sam," he said, handing me a novel, "look at the title of this book. It's a hoot." "*Albertine in the Lions' Den*," I read, "The Story of a Parisian Experiment in Infidelity." "Infidelity in Paris would certainly be more exciting than dipsy-doodling around northeast Connecticut," I said. "Gallantry hereabouts is so dull I've almost quit." "Sam," a woman then said, "one of your books is for sale upstairs on the landing. You should autograph it." I climbed the stairs and found *The Best of Pickering*. Years ago I had signed the book for someone named "Nikki." "What the hell," I muttered. "I might as well autograph the book again." "Whoever buys this book will never need an operation for piles," I wrote, after which I signed my name under which I wrote the date 22 October, 2011. I walked back downstairs and started perusing books. Almost immediately I noticed *Everything You Always Wanted To Know About Sex*. I opened the book to the title page and under the title wrote, "I don't want to know one goddamn thing more about sex." I then placed the book back on the display table and walked away. I bought one book at the sale, *Chips Off the Old Benchley*, a collection of Robert Benchley's occasional essays. On the spine of the book appeared a sketch of Benchley's face, a cartoon depicting a pudgy man wearing a top hat and a bow tie, a flower in his buttonhole. I showed the sketch to the woman who took the dollar I paid for the book. "This is my kind of book," I said. "I'm damn tired of reading about the inspirational aspirations of the lower classes." Vicki overheard me. "What has gotten into you?" she asked. "You are behaving worse than usual." "You'd act this way, too, if you'd seen the Bonassus," I said. "Bonassus, my assus. Let's go to Willimantic and have lunch at Café Mantic. A chocolate tart will hit the spot and settle you down," she said seizing my free hand. "Okay," I said, suddenly remembering two sentences in Max Beerbohm's *Yet Again*. "The age of miracles is not past. But I would raise no false hopes of myself."

Shopping

The day after school ended, Vicki and I ate lunch at Panera. Afterward we shopped. My appetite for possessions has vanished, and I didn't purchase anything. At Coldwater Creek Vicki bought a gray jacket smacking of the Outback. While she roamed racks of clothes, I rusticated in an easy chair. A basket sat atop a table on my right. Piled high in the basket was a shingle of smooth palm-sized beach stones. Imported from Indonesia, the stones sold for $5.95 apiece. Printed on them in black letters were uplifting, therapeutic words, among others, Love, Gratitude, Serenity, Imagine, Laugh, Enjoy, and Relax. The stones did not inspire me. Instead they awakened recollections of boyhood. The stones were ideal for rock battles. If thrown side-armed, they'd plane through the air and rise, making them difficult to dodge. "Pow, wham, thwack—that's what should be printed on them," I told a clerk, "the sound of a rock hammering smush into a collar bone or blapping a chin into a tantrum of blood." "I'll never shop with you again," Vicki said as she pulled me out of the store. "When you demonstrated the technique for, as you called it, 'maximizing effective throwing,' leaning over and whipping your arm around, I thought the poor woman was going to call the police."

Although I rarely buy anything, my shopping cart is overflowing. Almost every day an acquaintance rattles an item into it. Last month an old friend wrote to tell me she had become a lesbian. She worried about my reaction. She should not have been concerned. "All right-thinking people prefer women to men," I replied. "I always have." Another friend e-mailed the literary editor of a conservative magazine and recommended me as a columnist. Eighteen minutes later the editor replied, rejecting me, saying my writings reminded him of those of Wendell Berry. "Extraordinary praise by criticism or in religious terms salvation through damnation," I said to Vicki. Then, of course, whenever I reach the weekly check-out counter, I usually discover an unexpected letter. "Professor Pickering," Frederick wrote recently, "My sending this comes as a surprise to me. I am not much of a reader, but I was in the grocery store yesterday fetching things my wife asked me to get and nearing a bill of $25. The store also sells gasoline, and if one purchases $25 or more in goods he will receive 5 cents off for each gallon of gas he buys—up to 20 gallons. Lacking a dollar to reach my $25 goal, I saw a stack of books on sale, two for $4. I chose *Letters to a Teacher* and another book. I have read about half your book. I must say it is the most relaxing book I have read in a very long time. Well done. Frederick."

Despite the "hands-on" demonstration in Coldwater Creek, my cart contains few ligaments or shards of bone. Rarely do I stray from the softly domestic. In fact most things in my cart were tossed in by Vicki, a laundry of shirts, for example. Every holiday Vicki gives me a checkered shirt, usually red and blue or green and gray, saying, "You dress like a bag man." "But I like looking raggedy," I invariably answer, "disheveled becomes me." Three months ago she changed her delivery and pitched in Binky, a Chihuahua rescued from a breeding pen in Arkansas. Binky had spent life in a cage being bred and giving birth. As a result she has been a project. When she first appeared, she was frightened of almost everything—stairs, puddles, and birds. Binky weighs only seven pounds, but I have lost muscle mass. When her weight is added to that of the two other rescue dogs, Jack's ten and a half pounds and Suzy's eleven and a half, the clump is practically too great for me to push through.

No longer does a ferry run from Maine to Nova Scotia. To reach Four Winds, our house in Beaver River, we now must drive to New Brunswick, spend a night in St. John, and the next day take the *Princess of Acadia* ferry to Digby, after which we have to drive another eighty miles to the southwest. The distance from Storrs to our motel in St. John was 526 miles, a long way for a ragged man to transport a kennel. During the two days we walked the dogs nine times, first at the "Welcome to Maine" rest stop just north of the Piscataqua River, second beside a Burger King on Interstate 95 south of Portland, and third in a mosquito haven somewhere along the barrens between Bangor and Calais. At our motel we walked the dogs four times, twice at night, once when we arrived and again before bed, and twice the next morning, before and after breakfast. Before driving onto the *Princess of Acadia*, we walked the dogs yet again, this time along the bay near the ferry terminal. On arriving in Nova Scotia, I pulled into a lay-by outside Digby and walked the dogs for the last time. All the stopping and starting the car, attaching and detaching leashes, feeding and watering, plucking droppings from the ground, and the unceasing refrain "Do your business" exhausted me, and I arrived in Beaver River drooping and practically panting.

Soon, however, I felt better. My eyes picked a welcoming bouquet of flowers, turning my cart into a florist bucket: candied rugosa roses, dame's rocket, and leggy buttercups dipping and rising, churning in a sea breeze. Yellow melted and ran through the long-veined sepals of blue flag, while the keels of lupin looked like the deep wells of biblical lamps, above them pink flaring in flames. The indented globes of sheep laurel revolved around twiggy spindles, and peppermint sticks of white, yellow, and pink fragrance turned honey suckle into a sweet shop. Behind the flowers I spread a ruffle of cinnamon ferns, the stalks of fertile leaves honeyed and wreathed with spore cases.

Life's intriguing mazes delight youth. Straight aisles and simple habits appeal more to the aged. Time sands away belief, leaving behind not a plain smooth with answers but moody impatience with complexity. Clarity appeals to me more than it did in the past. No longer do I have the patience to seine through yellows and greens in order to differentiate one warbler from another. Instead the sight of an eider cheers, indeed invigorates, me, most of its feathers so black and white they seem opinionated. Every summer in Nova Scotia the items in my basket are familiar. Vicki and I eat western sandwiches and fish chowder at the Quick 'n Tasty. We drink medium-sized cups of coffee and munch Timbits at Tim Hortons. At Comeau's Market in Meteghan we buy raspberries. At D. J.'s in Salmon River, we pick up chocolate cake, and in Port Maitland brown bread at Edna Churchill's bakery. I eat so much that Vicki gives me an onomatopoetic nickname, this summer "Humptafee." Because the shelves I wander past are similar summer after summer, I occasionally revolt, spilling the refinement of sugary propriety. On learning that Eric had a stent inserted into an artery in May, I telephoned him. "Nanine told me you have a stent," I said. "She wasn't sure whether it had been rammed into your heart or behind. All I can say is that I would like to see it if it is in one of those two places." Eric had not expected my call, and his reply was politely impacted. "Neither," he said, "in an artery." Time upsets the contents of people's baskets. For several years Eric and I were two of the three members of a men's triathlon team. We participated in the Yarmouth Triathlon and always finished second, except for one summer when three men's teams entered the competition and we finished third. Eric was the swimmer, and the stent, no matter its placement, torpedoed our team.

At times I didn't recognize the contents of my basket. During the past year Mr. Brown rebuilt the chimney to which the wood stove in the kitchen is attached. The chimney runs through the ceiling of the kitchen and passes through our bedroom above. In the past, cooking heated the bricks and kept the bedroom warm. Fire codes have changed since the chimney was built in the 1950s, forcing Mr. Brown to insert a flame-retardant pipe into the chimney. Now, no matter how hot the fire in the stove the bedroom remains chilly. Although a chimney fire no longer threatens to cremate us, some nights I imagine our becoming icicles.

Vicki rarely buys a single item. A first cereal, for example, attracts a second cereal, and by the time she reaches the cash register at Sobey's, her cart contains boxes of All Bran, Alpen, Just Right, Shredded Wheat, and Weetabix's GrainShop. Similarly after seeing a first bouquet, I saw another, this one composed of boutonnières evoking the wilted past and not blooming bright in the weedy present, a memento mori consisting of locks of hair woven into flowers. The bouquet was old, having been begun in the 1860s. Family members snipped hair from the heads of dead relatives and wove them into flowers. The bouquet was large and had blossomed through at least four generations. A few blooms were gray, but one hundred and fifty years ago, many people died young, and several flowers were brown or black. One was red. Daisies were the most popular flower although weavers frequently wove vines, their tendrils curling and clutching stems of the daisies, resembling Virginia creeper. As I studied the bouquet, I imagined matching blossoms and personalities—bull thistle for a crotchety, acerbic old man, bake apple for a beloved aunt who cooked tables of pies for family reunions, "the best pies in Digby County," maiden pink for a "lassie" who died before puberty, and lily of the valley for a distant cousin who lived and died almost anonymously, her days spent quietly feeding squirrels and chipmunks deep in a spruce forest. If only sweet William had stumbled upon her rustic cottage like the fairy tale's Prince Charming, her life would have been glorious, babies in her lap and children smiling at her knees, a life very different from that led by her sister false nettle who ran away to Halifax and whose tarnished doings were never mentioned in the presence of family members younger than forty. Although Mayflower and Mayweed were twins, they were different, the former becoming a school teacher, the latter a banker. If Vicki stopped buying me shirts, ragged Robin would suit me, I thought. The bouquet in my mind was capacious with space for green field blossoms: forget-me not, shooting star, sweet Cicely, almost every flower except butterfly pea.

Last Saturday we drove to the farmer's market in Yarmouth. By the time we arrived, Natalie had sold out of scones. "Except that one," I said, pointing to a basket. "I can't sell that," Natalie said. "I found a hair from my little dog on it." Years of owning small dogs had made me immune to canine effluvia. "I'm the high priest of petite bow-wows," I said, adding that if all the dog hair I'd swallowed were balled into yarn a seamstress could weave a cassock. "Well," Natalie said. "I can't sell the scone, but I can give it away. Would you like it?" "Yes," I said. Hunks of rhubarb seasoned the scone, and I ate it later that morning in Tim Hortons. The scone bucked me up so much that I felt bold enough to repeat a tale I'd heard at the university graduation to Vicki, one of those stories that sophisticates label the last of pea time, the first of frost. "If you can guess what's in my hand," a wag said to a farmer, "I will give it to you, and you can make an omelet." "Describe it," the farmer said rubbing his chin. "It's white on the outside and yellow on the inside," the man said. "Well, that's an easy one," the farmer replied. "It's a hollow turnip stuffed with hunks of carrot."

For a person my age, shopping, indeed life itself, is predictable. When Vicki and I walked into Little Lebanon ten days ago, Peter looked over the counter and immediately said, "Two vegetarian extras, a pot of anise tea, and a Pepsi with ice." I'm not sure why I don't switch aisles and careening recklessly fill my cart with different items. I suspect that I have grown comfortable with the comfortable. At the end of June, Vicki and I celebrated our 32nd wedding anniversary in a familiar, reassuring way. We drove to the Fish Market in Meteghan for lunch, eating scallop burgers and splitting a Coca Cola. Next we went to Frenchy's, a used clothing store, and Vicki bought two blankets for the dogs and a red and green checkered shirt for me. While she shopped, I stayed in the car and fell asleep. As we left the parking lot, I noticed three other aging husbands sitting in cars, all asleep, heads cranked back and mouths open. From Frenchy's we drove along the bay to Comeau's Market, and Vicki picked up beet greens for dinner. On the return to Beaver River, we stopped at the Tim Hortons in Meteghan. We drank medium coffees in ceramic mugs and split a chocolate cake doughnut iced with chocolate. "A perfect day," I said. "You know," Vicki said, "people stay in prison longer than we have been married." "Good for them," I said. At dusk a song sparrow perched atop the last remaining post of our clothes line. Music bubbled from him in a jubilee. "An oldie," Vicki said, patting me on the shoulder.

Tarry

In Digby I parked at the end of the wharf outside the Royal Fundy seafood restaurant. The Royal Fundy was familiar, walls, tables, and oilcloth all blue and white, the seafood fresh almost hung with rockweed and kelp. Vicki and I sipped Rudder's Red Ale and ate scallop burgers and sweet potato fries. For dessert we split a piece of rhubarb-raspberry pie. Ahead lay the drive down the French Coast to Beaver River. We had spent two days on the road, and the sun was sliding down the horizon. We were not in a hurry, however. We have become dawdlers and grown accustomed to lingering over meals. Every Tuesday Vicki and I drive to Yarmouth and have "High Tea by the Sea" at Holy Trinity Anglican Church. Church members serve platters of sandwiches, the crust sliced off: salmon, egg salad, potted ham, tuna fish, and one week cucumber and cream cheese, the next cherry and cream cheese. In the middle of tables sit scones and jams, usually apricot and strawberry. Dessert trays resemble bakery shelves: uncooked balls rolling with chocolate and walnuts, mince meat tarts, raspberry squares, fudge, fruit cake, and marshmallows hollowed and crammed with maraschino cherries then toasted in coconut.

Vicki and I loiter, sipping and tasting. After tea we make our weekly trip to the laundromat. While our clothes slosh about, we stroll Water Street and look at the sailboats tied to Killiam Wharf. Sometimes we go to the library, and I check out a handful of books, this past week *High Tide in Tucson*, a collection of Barbara Kingsolver's essays, *Out of Eden*, a study of feral "ecological invasions," and Augusten Burroughs' memoir of childhood *Running with Scissors*. To palliate the bilious aftertaste of Burroughs' book, I also borrowed the biography of the

Yorkshire veterinarian, James Herriot, written by his son James Wright, its pages as bland as baking soda. From the library we go to the Tim Hortons and top off tea with coffee and two Timbits apiece. On sunny days I wear a Panama hat. Townspeople don't know us, but they recognize the hat and nod. "Do you think anybody will write your biography?" Vicki asked, munching a maple Timbit and looking at Wright's book. "You have written millions of words." "No," I said. "I'm humdrum. My days have been too easy, and my life is an open magazine." Besides, I continued, emending a statement made by Charles Brooks in the twenties, "if anybody ever reads one of my books, he reads it in secret like the Bible." "Too bad," Vicki said, swallowing a last nibble of maple. "Time to head back to the laundromat." "Off we go," I said, pushing away from the table, standing up slowly, and putting on my hat.

Today's child is tomorrow's young man. In contrast age is dormant. In the old, change occurs gradually, except, of course, for the final steep decline. Time turns even the most protean into a tarrier. Age also alters the immune system. One becomes addicted to pondering and allergic to certainty. When matters become burdensome, age follows the advice of the old saw, "When you can't stand things, sit down." For the tarrier the best stories are, from youth's perspective, ponderously slow. Before I left Storrs this summer, Josh dropped by the house. A student, he recounted, had come to his office that morning. "Professor Gasden is a wonderful scholar," the student said. "Is she?" Josh replied. "Oh, yes," the student gushed, "I asked her why she preferred Virginia Woolf's novels to those of Jane Austen." "What did she say?" Josh said. "She said she didn't know why," the student answered. "Interesting, refreshingly perceptive," Josh said. "Yes, indeed, Professor Gasden is a splendid and original scholar, a nonpareil."

"Finally brethren," St. Paul said to the Philippians, "whatsoever things are true, whatsoever things are honest, whatsoever things are just, whatsoever things are pure, whatsoever things are lovely, whatsoever things are of good report; if there be any virtue, and if there be any praise, think on these things." I read Paul's epistle on the fourth of July, a day that some time ago I dedicated to pondering my independence from the lower social virtues like patriotism. Mulling comes more easily to those moored in the shelter of age than it does for the ambitious, forever tossed about in the sea of mutability. No harbor is secluded enough to exclude all fashionable currents, however. The next morning the Halifax newspaper pushed St. Paul to the rocky edge of mind. Ten pictures of Kate Middleton, the young wife of Prince William, heir to the British crown, appeared in the paper. All the pictures were in color. Two were on the front page, and another on page three. Three pictures appeared on the first page of section E, and four more on page four. "Gee," I said, dropping the paper and picking up *USA Weekend*, an insert that had lain on the kitchen table for a week. The feature article described President Obama's personal trainer. I hadn't met anyone who had a personal trainer. "Californication," I said, handing the *Weekend* to Vicki. "Forget it," Vicki said tossing the insert into the recycle box. "Kate and William, the President of the United States are television-made. They are mayflies, created by journalism, fluttering in the sunlight today, but moldy shells tomorrow. Remember the story of Apsethus and be wise." According to Hippolytus, Apsethus wanted people to think him a god, so he caught hundreds of parrots and taught them to say "Aspethus is a god." Afterward he released the parrots across Libya. When people heard the parrots speak, they assumed that a miracle had occurred. Believing that Nature herself was addressing them, they began to treat Apsethus as a god. Apsethus's divinity lasted until a Greek became suspicious and gathered his own flock of parrots and taught them to recite, "Apsethus caged us and forced us to say that Aspethus was a god." On the release of this second flock of parrots, public opinion turned against Apsethus. The populace became enraged, rose up, and burned him alive. "Celebrity is a candle with a short wick," Vicki continued. "Go back to reading the Bible." "Okay," I said, "but first a heeltap of the warming south. As an elder I am bound to follow Paul's advice in his *Epistle to Timothy* and 'use a little wine' for my 'stomach's sake' and 'other infirmities.'"

For the dawdler days are pageants. The slow life is never empty, and dawdlers notice white admiral butterflies atop cymes of wild raisin, pools of daisies splashed across a drumlin above the Gulf of Maine, and a primrose moth head down in the blossom of an evening primrose, the forewing pink nearest the head but turning yellow like the flower's petals nearer the apex and outer margin. The dawdler hears gulls squeezing themselves into raucous blares, notices the green, thumb-sized caterpillar of a fawn sphinx moth, minute spines thorny along its blue horn, and in a scrub of broken spruce, spots a Swainson's thrush, its call note chipping at the flaking bark. Cooling one's heels warms hours. From a carpet of white clover wrinkled across a disturbed slope on Black Point perfume rose in a melody that made me dance even though my feet did not move. Every summer the old rosebay rhododendron beside the barn seems willful, twigs and branches crochet hooks thick and impenetrable, white and pink blossoms sometimes knitted over its leaves, other times like this year the blossoms thin and tired, dangling loose as yarn.

Tarrying fosters digression. On ambles recently I've thought about friendship. Friendship depends upon shared language, not simply words and their pronunciation but also the tales they tell. Perhaps I have spent so much time in the natural world observing birds and flowers as compensation from straying from the familial South. Maybe most people who study nature are loners, tarriers who have wandered from their childhoods. Because easterners misunderstand, I have told the majority of my stories only to the page. Oh, well, enough digression—folks tell me that the big boys talk a lot about me in Washington and also, of course, in Moscow. I wonder what they say. Vicki thinks the conversation stems from my being misquoted in the *Washington Post*, saying that banishing a priest from the sanctuary for marrying a woman was understandable, but defrocking him for marrying a man "was contrary to all reason and tradition."

Tarriers sip the lees of life. "Though much is taken, much abides," Tennyson's Ulysses said, exhorting his aged comrades to abandon Ithaca and smiting the sounding furrows "sail beyond the sunset." As sunset slides striated across the horizon, most people furl their sails and relax into tarrying. The pleasures of sundry races are to the slow and homebound, not the swift, their vision pinched by intention. Dawdlers do not become a part of all that they meet. Instead they enjoy many entertaining days. When, in Tennyson's words, "the vessel puffs her sail," I drift into the happy doldrums. At the end of July, Vicki and I drove to Barrington, "The Lobster Capital of Canada," and I ran the Nova Scotia Half Marathon. Because I am stutteringly slow, I chatted with a score of runners: a Swedish biologist attending a conference on mercury in Halifax, a banker from Albany on the last day of his vacation, and an officer in the Department of Fisheries and Oceans who had studied naval engineering but who could not endure oily days below deck. Because I have a southern accent, people often assume I am a political recidivist. "What do you think about our socialist government here in Nova Scotia?" a man asked in a disgruntled voice. "Not too goddamn much," I replied, pausing to allow the man to nod in agreement. "I'm a communist, and they don't go far enough."

"You sure told him," Vicki said after the race when I repeated the conversation. "What was I supposed to say?" I replied. "I could have told him that some folks call lilies of the valley ladders to heaven or that creeping Jenny is sometimes dubbed herb twopence because its leaves appear in pairs, round as pennies. Maybe I should have quoted Ecclesiastes, 'The thing that hath been, it is *that* which shall be; and that which is done *is* that which shall be done: and *there* is no new thing under the earth.' Or better, perhaps I should have quoted Leigh Hunt:

> Jenny kissed me when we met,
> Jumping from the chair she sat in;
> Time, you thief, who love to get
> Sweets into your list, put that in;
> Say I'm weary, say I'm sad,
> Say that health and wealth have missed me
> Say I'm growing old, but add,
> Jenny kissed me."

"Enough," Vicki said, quoting Tennyson herself. "You ran a good race. It's too late to seek a newer world. Let's eat." Lunch was an odyssey. We began with fish chowder at the Barrington Curling Club, ladled out for us by Peter an hour before a complimentary meal was scheduled to be served to runners and their families. Afterward we drove Route 3 along the South Shore passing through the sleepy inlets of Lower East Pubnico, Mid East Pubnico, East Pubnico, West Pubnico, and Mid West Pubnico. Eventually we docked at the Dennis Point Café in Lower West Pubnico where we ate creamed lobster sandwiches. Then we tacked back to Yarmouth, stopping at Tim Hortons on Starrs Road. There we drank coffee and ate chocolate chip muffins. "Sixteen grams of fat and four hundred and thirty calories," Vicki said biting into her muffin, "more seductive than Circe and more dangerous to your health than the Cyclops." "Yes, despite all the palaver about 'roaming with a hungry heart,' Ulysses never had a day as good as this," I said, "and, oh, before I forget, did you know that another name for garlic mustard is Jack by the hedge?"

"Self-consciousness," Malcolm Gladwell wrote, "is the enemy of interestingness." Tarriers are not particularly self-conscious. Power doesn't seduce them, and the opinions of others rarely matter. Four times a week I jog eight miles circling Cedar Lake. A real dawdler, not an amateur like me, has decorated his house on the Beaver River Road. Knick-knacks attract Vicki, and several years ago at Canadian Tire she bought two trolls, Jens and Olaf. During the summer she shifts them from room to room, placing them near windows "so they will be able to see us and the dogs outside and won't be lonely." Nevertheless Vicki thinks the man on the Beaver River Road has gone too far. For my part I admire his handiwork and hope he has just begun. On a bank sloping toward the road are two raised flower beds, literally beds, their heads and footboards removed from brass bedsteads, the side rails logs. Planted in the beds are pans of funkia, day lilies, and cowlicks of ornamental grass. Pasted to the house itself are four brown plastic stars, three large and one small. Lining the walk leading from the driveway to the front stoop are six handles from well pumps. Two lions crouch beside the stoop, not full-sized lions like those that roam the Kalahari but miniature lions, similar to miniature horses, playthings found in paddocks in California. In the yard appear four replicas of the old Yarmouth Lighthouse, all painted in red and white vertical stripes. Near the entrance to the driveway stands a pair of wishing wells, complete with buckets. Atop five pedestals sit silver globes, crosses between disco lamps and the crystal balls of fortune tellers. From another pedestal three balls rise on tines looking like an upside-down pawnbroker's sign. Strings of lights wrap all the pedestals in the yard. Here and there are bird baths, a pink flamingo pruning itself beside the tallest bath. In a corner of the yard a concrete squirrel four feet tall rears up, standing on its back legs and staring aggressively at the road. A life-sized doe stands demure under a maple; nailed to the tree is a sign reading "No Hunting." Herds of deer frolic across yards in Yarmouth County; the species vary, some plastic, others plaster or concrete. Although the deer are pets and are almost always protected by "No Hunting" signs, many are pocked by shell holes.

Sometimes dawdlers carry their penchant for decoration to an extreme. Near the end of August, I bought a child-sized grapenuts ice cream cone at Comeau's Market. I sat outside the market in a red Adirondack chair, licking and watching traffic when a burly man lumbered past. The man had decorated his body, not his yard. He wore a wife-beater. His arms and shoulders were conventional graveyards of skulls while a den of snakes slithered over his collarbones and coiled around his neck. He had shaved his head, however, and had gone a trifle over the top, at least for my taste, having a motorcycle tattooed across his neurocranium, for the record a Kawasaki, not a Harley-Davidson, the usual ornamental sidecar of snakes and skulls.

Some dawdlers make extraordinary efforts and linger longer than expected. On Sunday evenings the Yarmouth radio station CJLS devotes thirty minutes to the People's Gospel Hour. The broadcast features a sermon by Pastor Perry F. Rockwood. Last Sunday Perry attacked "Devilvision," or as the woebegone know it, television. The sermon was lively and sensible, my only caveat being that the good pastor died three years ago, his loitering on the airwaves almost smacking too much of the "Lazarusene." Nevertheless, only fools ignore warnings from the grave, and I winced on hearing, "So many professional people are lost and on the way to Hell, and so many university professors." My discomfort was short-lived. Vicki spoke, and I slipped back into the cozy equilibrium of the doomed. "Did you ever think you were among the damned?" Vicki asked. "Certainly, I've sniffed the piquant incense of brimstone in the halls outside my classroom for decades." In any case tomb chatter is often so entertaining that the aroma of sulfur doesn't linger. At the conclusion of the program, Perry quoted a lawyer who told him, "I might have been a Christian if I had not met so many who said they were."

The lives of dawdlers are endlessly rich. A fortnight ago Josh sent me a limerick he found in a forgotten magazine. "A delight," he wrote, "a poem to ponder during the midnight hour."

> Alf Alford, who lives down at Alpha,
> Has raised a large crop of Alfalfa.
> But those who would buy,
> Find it no use to try
> To get Alf's Alfalfa at Alpha.

Many dawdlers are sentimentalists. They think more about the past and ignoring the present don't meddle and disrupt. Instead of railing against the moment, they indulge in pleasing melancholy. On Monday I shelled peas. The woodstove was ablaze, the firebox exuding the homey aroma of maple and birch. In the meadow outside the kitchen a robin bounced across the grass, searching for worms to feed a fledgling nesting in the golden elder beside the backhouse. I sat at the kitchen table. For almost twenty years, Eliza sat beside me, and we shelled peas together. Occasionally a pea popped from a pod and rolled across the floor. It did not roll far. Penny, our pea hound as we called her, always scooped it up. Penny is now dead, buried beside a boulder in Connecticut, and Eliza is in Berlin. For a moment shelling seemed inexpressively sad, and I ached to return to the past. I imagined tarrying through the childhoods of Eliza and Edward and Francis again. I do not want to linger beyond the grave like Pastor Perry. "Maybe I have dawdled hereabouts too long," I said to Vicki. "Rubbish. Sip this," Vicki said, handing me a glass of Gato Negro. "Now tell me about your plans to dry snow and market it as salt and to glue bristles on the tails of rats and sell them as squirrels for Brunswick stew." "Does it matter that I lifted the ideas from the pages of other dawdlers," I said. "Of course not," Vicki said.

The Last Exam

I've spent 65 years in school starting at four when I entered kindergarten. The time has come for me to leave the classroom. I'm living on the Hallelujah side of life as the gospel song puts it. When I wake early in the morning, my hands are dank and feel like cold sheets. My neck aches, and I perch for a minute or two on the side of the bed trying to master the pain before I put my feet on the floor. I am still an adequate teacher, "the best in the university," a student said recently. The old are suckers for superlatives, and I appreciated the exaggeration. My aggies haven't rolled out the door, and my sentences still spiral and corkscrew with color. Still, I worry that my cat's-eyes have begun to blink. Twice during the past month after I boiled water in order to make tea I forgot to turn off the burner. Too many academic careers drift into the smudge of soft lead and softer thought. Better it is to seize an eraser and rub one's presence away before blots mar the cursive running of days.

For one thing time has affected my appreciation of books. Once, the subtle attracted me, stories and poems that demanded explicators, that is, teachers. Nowadays simplicity appeals more to me, writing that any reader can enjoy and which instead of being the catalyst for understanding makes a person smile and perhaps if he is feeling lively leads him to mouth "gee." At the Mansfield Library book sale in October, I bought a ratty copy of Thornton Burgess's *The Adventures of Old Mr. Toad*. I purchased the book because the beginning of the first chapter, "Jimmy Skunk is Puzzled," made me happy. "Old Mother West Wind," Burgess wrote, "had just come down from the Purple Hills and turned loose her children, the Merry Little Breezes, from the big bag in which she had been carrying them. They were very lively as they danced and raced across the Green Meadows in all directions, for it was good to be back there once more. Old Mother West Wind almost sighed as she watched them for a few minutes. She felt that she would like to join them. Always the springtime made her feel this way—young, mad, carefree, and happy."

I have long liked John Masefield's tales of adventure, and at the sale when I saw a copy of *Sard Harker*, I picked it up, paying a dollar, twice what I paid for *Old Mr. Toad*. In contrast to lives not crinkled by age, old books and old people often surprise. The Mansfield Center Library Association purchased *Sard Harker* in 1924. Pasted inside the back cover of the book was a card measuring two by three and half inches. Printed on the card were the library hours, three to five Tuesday and Thursday afternoons and Saturday in the evening from seven-thirty to nine. Also on the card were rules for borrowing. For the most part the rules were conventional. Unless stamped "One Week Book," books could be borrowed for a fortnight, the fine levied for returning a book late being one cent a day. The last rule on the card, however, surprised me. "In case of contagious disease in family of book-taker, notify librarian before book is returned."

The rule was preventative. The influenza epidemic at the end of the First World War and diseases like measles and polio were probably its source, vaccinations for these last not having been created yet. Rarely do statements that surprise me smack of forgotten realities. Instead they are lesser remarks, startling and delighting but then quickly dropping from mind, aphorisms such as "The early worm gets the beak" and "Writers begin by composing and end by decomposing." Frequently I write down statements and stuff them into my desk. As a result, scraps of paper clutter my study. The bits resemble toppled tombstones. The writing on them remains out of sight, being read only when I transform myself into a groundskeeper and mulch the contents of my study. Last week I threw away a bag of jottings, only one of which I remember, "'Easy come, easy go' doesn't apply to cancer, pregnancy, or freckles."

Scraps are weedy and have deep taproots. No matter the rigor of my mowing they send shoots through my study, especially in winter when I don't prune as often as during summer. In Atlanta recently I overheard a man describe a potential employee. "He is very religious, but that shouldn't cause concern," the man said, adding after a pause, "He also has a good character." Years of teaching have shaped my life, turning class routine into habit. As I scribble in the margins of student essays, so I jot down notes about doings outside school, something retirement probably won't change. In contrast to comments on student papers, my observations off the page don't suggest changes or improvements. They are just observations.

My pocketbook is too shallow to pay for hotel meals, and in Atlanta, I ate breakfast at the White House Café on Peachtree Road. Next to the café was Brazilian Wax by Andreia. Brazilian Wax, I wrote down, had been "Voted Best in Atlanta." Waxing was "Available for Men." Moreover, a sign declared, Andreia was running a thirty-five dollar special. The sign did not say, however, what parts or how much of a person the special covered, or more accurately uncovered, leaving me matter to mull as I strolled along Peachtree after breakfast. I had gone to Atlanta to speak at a luncheon. Because the number of speakers grew unexpectedly, my talk shrank from fifteen to five minutes. My expenses amounted $880.73, including, among other things, air fare, hotel, breakfast at the White House, and $3.06 to purchase toothpaste after Homeland Security confiscated my tube of Crest at the security check point in Hartford. Each minute I spoke, I emphasized at the beginning of my talk, cost $174.13, each second $2.90. "Only a financial ninny," I said, "would ignore such pricy words."

I drew no conclusion from the actuarial pondering. Indeed almost never do my observations suggest conclusions, putting me out of step with the contemporary university, managers of which spend semesters relentlessly assessing and mailing questionnaires pocked with phrases like "Program Mission" and "Learning Outcome Statement." Books do not mirror life, but occasionally a story instructs. I ignore assessments, the lesson of "Brother Rabbit Secures a Mansion" in *Nights with Uncle Remus* having influenced my view of measuring. In the story the creatures "tuck a notion" to go into cahoots and build a house. After saying that climbing a scaffold made his head swim and that working in the sun gave him palsy, Brer Rabbit picked up a square, stuck a pencil behind his ear, and went "'roun' medjun' en markin.'" He was so busy the other creatures said that he was doing a monstrous sight of work and folks going along the road thought he was working harder than all the rest of the animals put together. "Yit all de time," Uncle Remus recounted, "Brer Rabbit aint doin' nothin', en he des well bin layin' off in the de shade scratchin' de fleas off'n 'im."

"A lady" once offered Thoreau a mat for his cabin at Walden Pond. Thoreau refused the present, explaining he had no time to spare to shake the mat. He said he preferred wiping his feet on the sod before the door, adding, "It is best to avoid the beginnings of evil." Beginnings that my students think useful, and intriguing, I often think nuisances. I don't own a cell phone and am not curious about iPods and blackberries of the non-fruit variety. Almost never do I use the telephone at home, and when it rings, I often leave the room until the cacophony stops. Age has made me a solitary. People and sad lives that flare burning across days like blisters have made me weary. Students still delight me, however, and after I retire, I will regret their absence. Last fall classes made me aware of a culturally-significant hormone change, estrogen shifting from women to men and testosterone from men to women. One morning I conducted a transportation survey, the results of which revealed that the sexes differ greatly from what they were when I was in college. Of the fifty-eight students in my courses, six girls drove Jeeps. Not one boy drove a Jeep. "Keeping safe and minding their highway manners in little pink Camry's," a girl who drove a thunderously big pick-up truck said. Despite the survey, not for decades has a student said or written anything that startled me into ruminating about the future. In contrast students have often awakened memory, and in their presence the past quickens, making me aware of how wondrous life has been.

Early in the 1960s when I was an undergraduate, I spent summers working as a camp counselor in Raymond, Maine. Years later I sent my boys to the camp. Francis spent five years there, and Edward eleven as a camper and a counselor, while Eliza attended the sister camp on Sebago Lake. This past semester when I mentioned the camp in passing, Sarah immediately asked, "What is the name of the camp?" Her father and uncle had gone to the same camp while Sarah went to the girls' camp. Suddenly I smelled pines trees and thought about friends whom I had not seen in forty-five years. "Old Chief Timanous was a camper and king," I sang. "And the kind of man that campers ought to be," Sarah said, finishing the line.

"What grade does Sarah have now?" Vicki asked that evening when I described my "happy day." I said she had a B. "Don't you give her an A- just because her father went to Timanous," Vicki said. "Certainly not. I'm not some thin-shanked, narrow-breasted Pentecostal," I replied. "I'm not going to give her an A- or for that matter a B+. I'm giving her an A." "Jesus," Vicki exclaimed, "the time has come for you to retire." "Maybe so," I said. "I just can't give a big goddamn about grades any longer."

Shrouds lack pockets, forcing corpses to travel light. Many aging people weigh themselves down with slights. For my part I have written twenty-five books and hundreds of articles. Each year the English Department puts together a panel for graduate students on publishing. Never have I been asked to be on the panel. Perhaps people don't want to bother me. Still, not being invited has irked me. The pettiness of allowing myself to be irritated, however, disturbs me more, and I must retire before imaginary slights manacle hours and sour appreciation of the sweet years I've spent at the university. In any case most of my friends have retired, old boys who wrote stylish books and who dallied genially, fellows who were responsible and decent, who drank milk from mad cows without barking and who swallowed inconsistencies without gagging and calling attention to themselves, teachers who never heard of learning outcomes but who worked hard and hoped for the best, although they didn't define *best* by distorting life and slamming it into a straightjacket so it could be measured.

Retirement isn't death, and, of course, teachers never throw off the moral coil. My desk contains bales of advice, most of which I'll gladly recycle, good sense like "Don't ever invite a fat woman to lean on your arm." To forestall misunderstanding, let me explain that by *fat* I mean a gal so big that it will take two clergymen and a boy to preach her funeral. Or if you think that advice unseemly, how about this: "If someone insults you, retort that you don't have enough confidence in his veracity to believe him." In any case despite planning to retire, I'm almost lively. Last month I ran the Hartford Half-Marathon, and Vicki said I looked good at the finish, "smiling and running straight up." "You're the man," she exclaimed, after which she slapped me on the back and said, "now give me a big kiss."

I ran easily because the day was cool and cousins of assessors were everywhere: the announcer at the start of the race, clearly blind because he repeatedly referred to all the runners as athletes, and then the woman holding a sign that read "You Are Your Inner Hero." "Horseshit," I muttered when I saw the sign. "Amen," a man chuffing next to me responded. At the halfway point, a banner stretched over the course reading "The Best Is Yet To Come." "Oh, dear," a woman said. I'll enjoy retirement because English teachers don't stop talking after they close the door to the classroom. In great part the run was easy because I chatted with people. A middle-aged couple sat on a curb in West Hartford and watched the race. "My God, you are married to a beautiful woman," I said to the husband. The wife smiled, and I skipped down the street. Whenever I felt tired, I drew alongside women of a certain age and said, "I'll bet you never expected to see Robert Redford running next to you." Four miles from the end of the race a woman told me she lived in Nashville, my birthplace. She had run a marathon in every state in the union, thirty-two marathons in the last year alone, and was treating the half-marathon as a training run. We talked about our children and parents, our homes and spouses. Her husband had pitched in the major leagues. Instead of squandering his salary, he bought property, selling out just before the recession. Her children were musical, and when I suggested that they should consider attending Sewanee, my old college, she said one of her boys had gone to summer music camp at Sewanee. Almost before I realized it, I crossed the finish line. After my eight o'clock class the following Monday a boy approached me. "You beat my friend by a second," the boy said. "All right," I said, rising onto my toes and jigging slightly while balling my right hand into a fist and pushing it back and forth like a piston. "By the way," I said as the boy turned to leave the room, "what relation is your uncle's brother to you if he is not your uncle?" "What?" the boy said, looking puzzled. "Think about it. Ask your father," I said and walked away. "Students will miss you," Vicki said at dinner that night. "Babe, what a nice gal you are," I said, taking Vicki's hand, "honey would blush in your presence."

Birthday

In September I will be seventy. I look forward to the day. I have devoted many years to reaching seventy. My jogging friends are all over seventy. I am eager to leave the pledge class and become a full brother, initiated in the secret ways of age. No man, however, is an operating theater entire unto himself. No one can endure the postulate years of his 60s without viewing some of the relics in the Temple of Methuselah. Last month I helped extract Fred from a hospital in Hartford. Fred could not walk by himself. When we reached Fred's house, I got down on all fours and crawled up the steps like a terrapin, Fred leaning on my back while Tom lifted his legs off the ground, first the right then the left. The next afternoon I visited Henry. Two months earlier a surgeon had pared through Henry's abdomen and minced a foot of colon. Henry was in good spirits and escorted me through a topographical tour of his scars, one of them deeper than Death Valley.

I have been an attentive neophyte. On David's 75th birthday I sent him a pink Sweet Sixteen card. "You look older than sixteen," I wrote, "but, as the life of Blind Bartimaeus shows, looks deceive. Our conversations have convinced me that intellectually this must be your sixteenth or maybe fifteenth birthday. Soon you will be able to get your driver's license. I know you are eager to get behind the wheel of a car. But be careful and go slow at first." On Harry's 76th birthday I sent him a 100th birthday card, saying that although I did not know his exact age I knew he was "damn old." "100 strikes me as close enough," I wrote. "Anyway Ocean State Job Lot doesn't sell cards celebrating 110th or 120th birthdays."

In June I ran the Iron Horse Half-Marathon in Simsbury, Connecticut. Nine hundred and eighteen people ran. At the conclusion I discovered that I was the second oldest runner. In fact only seven people sixty-five and older ran. "You were not running to beat other people or to achieve a time, but against Time itself," my friend Josh said later. "The answer to 'where have all the flowers gone' is clear—gone to compost piles." For my part my stamens are wobbly. I have lost petals, and lady bees no longer bumble about me. Still, I enjoyed the race. For much of the run Armand and I plodded along side by side, flipping through the pages of our lives and laughing. At 74 Armand was the oldest runner in the race. His knees were bad, and after eight miles I drifted ahead of him, reeling in, as competitors put it, seventy people. Josh is a sump pump of quotations. "Old soldiers may fade into nothingness," Josh said, paraphrasing Douglas MacArthur, "but runners' hips, hamstrings, ankles, and backsides just give way." For a moment Josh's remarks threatened to undermine my "runner's high," but then I thought about the English Department. Of the forty-five or so members in Storrs, nine are older than me. Instead of packing anthropologists off to the Caucasus Mountains to interview the world's oldest people, the *National Geographic* should send investigators to Storrs. Somewhere amid freshman composition with its low fat diet of simple sentences lurks the secret of immortality.

In my family birthdays are ignored. As no notice was taken of my 21st birthday, so my 70th birthday will pass unnoted. The previous evening I will read "The Night before Christmas" to myself. The poem's good spirits make me appreciate life. The next morning I'll go for a long jog, but Vicki and I will not celebrate the day. In truth, most days, Humpty Dumpty's unbirthdays, are rich with the unexpected. Last Tuesday I received a fatuous entertaining e-mail. "Beloved, this is Rev. Jonathan

Daniels, the spiritual counselor to late Mr. Mathew P. Allen. This is to inform you that Brother Allen made you a beneficiary in his Last Will and it is clearly stated on his Last Testament. This may appear unbelievable but it is only the truth and I am not asking anything in return and rest assured that this is real. Please, get back to me as soon as possible and I will explain further. Peace be with you." The next morning I talked to my cousin Sherry. Sherry is slightly older than me, and our conversation ran to the funereal. That afternoon I mailed her the deed to Lot Number 55 in Section 29 of Hollywood Cemetery in Richmond. Our grandmother had paid $600 "including Perpetual Care" for the plot on 1 September, 1948. The lot consisted of "approximately 190 superficial feet." Grandmother, Grandfather, and Sherry's father are buried in the plot, leaving room for three additional bodies. "This is my parting gift to you," I wrote. "Since Connecticut is backward and forbids a person from decaying in his backyard and supplying fodder for local varmints, I intend to be incinerated."

Two days ago I cleared a bookcase in my study intending to donate the contents to the Mansfield Library Book Sale. On a shelf I found a five by nine inch note card. Written in pencil on the card was "The Little Trout," a poem I copied thirty years ago from *The Child's Gem*, a book published around 1840 in Worcester, Massachusetts. The poem was cautionary, but like much that is cautionary, it delighted and awakened the dozing imagination.

> Dear mother, said a little fish,
> Pray, is not that a fly?
> I'm very hungry, and I wish
> You'd let me go and try.

Sweet innocent, the mother cried,
And started from her nook,
That horrid fly is put to hide
The sharpness of the hook!

Now as I've heard, this little trout
Was young and foolish too;
And so he thought he'd venture out
To see if it were true.

And round about the hook he play'd
With many a longing look,
And Dear me to himself he said,
I'm sure that's not a hook.

I can give one little pluck,
Let's see, and so I will;
So on he went, and lo! It stuck
Quite through his little gill!

And as he faint and fainter grew,
With hollow voice he cried,
Dear mother, if I'd minded you,
I need not now have died.

I won't disrupt the rational placidity of my birthday by shoveling up such profundity. Years ago after I realized that most answers were unsatisfactory, I stopped asking questions. I don't have any wisdom to impart. Moreover what I think clashes with present-day academic matters. At the beginning of the summer term, I ran across John, a former student. John told me he was taking a course in World Literature. "Gracious, how parochial," I exclaimed. "I suppose you are reading an Egyptian novel, poetry chanted by a tribe in the Balkans, and a translation of fragments discovered in the grasp of a terracotta soldier unearthed in China. You should be reading Connecticut literature—books describing New Britain, Willimantic, and Hartford. Instead of maundering on about doings in the shadow of the pyramids, you might get to know actual places and learn something about this world, and life."

No longer does the momentary excite me. I resemble the fellow in the old story who for want of anything better to say when he met a friend on the street asked, "What's the news?" "Haven't you heard?" the friend exclaimed. "War has broken out in Europe." "Well," the man answered, glancing up and studying the blue sky, "they certainly picked a fine day for it." Age has tempered my zeal for improvement, the years revealing that most improvements don't better but simply change. Occasionally, however, an account of research at the university startles me. In January an announcement described an "interdisciplinary initiative" in which apiarists and entomologists combined "their vast learning" in an attempt to cross honey bees with fireflies. "By enabling bees to work at night and thus double a year's yield of honey, such a cross," the announcement stated, "would be a boon to the state's economy and another example of the university's commitment to the financial wellbeing of Connecticut." The scientists, I have recently heard, are on the verge of success. So far they have not fashioned a bioluminescent honey bee, but they have created lightning bugs with stingers. "The next best thing," the governor declared.

Convention dictates that as a person ages he should concentrate his energies and jettison distracting pleasures. "The perplexity of life arises," G. K. Chesterton wrote, "from there being too many interesting things in it for us to be interested properly in any of them." Certainly the genteel are expected to withdraw from the more riotous aspects of the fleshly. Since I fit the traditional definition of a gentleman as one who never gives offense unintentionally, I have decided to behave properly and forswear grammar. In the privacy of my study, I will, of course, continue to practice conventional grammar occasionally. In public I will not mention the word or refer to any of its proletarian hangers-on, among others, semi-colon, gerund, preposition, and past participle. Giving up grammar will be easy because an antibody has long lurked in my bloodstream. Spelling and punctuation never concerned Mother. "People who ponder such low matters are contemptuous," she once said when I suggested that she employ periods in her correspondence. "If my not punctuating offends you," she said, "I have raised a cad." Recently I mentioned Mother's scorn for grammar to a graduate student. "Was she a modernist?" the student asked. "No," I replied, "an heiress."

I told family members not to give me birthday presents. I have done for others, however, what I have forbidden them to do for me. Three years ago after Francis got a job in Bristol, I bought him a new car. Last week as we were jogging, David said to me, "If you were a woman you would be impossible to live with." On the contrary, I am feminine in my devotion to fairness, women, of course, being higher-minded than men. What I did for one child I have always done for the others. After I purchased the car for Francis, I put aside money with which to buy cars for Edward and Eliza. Three months ago Eliza requested the money. She said she didn't want an automobile. After she explained that she needed the money to pay for expenses at the Free University of Berlin, I transferred the amount into her savings account. Last week I bought Edward a Hyundai station wagon. Vicki doesn't approve of these financial doings. She calls me "The Enabler." Largesse, she maintains, undermines initiative and cripples children by keeping them dependent. Vicki's choice of words is poor. Instead of The Enabler, she should call me The Disabler, not a usage I will correct because I have forsworn grammar. In any case two days after I purchased the car I received a stimulating un-birthday telephone call from Hyundai America. "May I speak to Samuel Piercing?" a woman asked. "Call back when you get the name right," I replied and dropped the phone back in its cradle.

Yesterday I heard a gospel singer on the radio declare that it would be a "happy day" on "the golden strand" when he heard Jesus say, "Shake hands with Mother again." For a moment the song's longing melancholy threatened to become viral. But then I glanced out the window. A boy on a skateboard hurried along the sidewalk in front of the house. Strapped to his shoulders was a bright red backpack and on his head a blue baseball cap. His right foot rested on the board, and he used his left to push forward, slapping the pavement, almost clapping gleefully. "Damn straight," I said. Ten minutes later I'd entered the New Haven Labor Day Road Race and booked a two-night stay in the Omni Hotel. "A birthday present for us," I said that evening to Vicki. "We'll visit museums and eat continuously. I'll finish last in the race, but that doesn't matter. I'm almost seventy, and we'll have a crackerjack time."

When Found

"When found, make a note of," Captain Cuttle advised in *Dombey and Son*. "Quite right," I thought jotting down Samuel Smiles's statement that cheerfulness and diligence were "nine-tenths of practical wisdom." "They are," Smiles wrote in *Self-Help*, "the life and soul of success, as well of happiness." On the cusp of retirement, I knew I'd miss the affectionate comedy of the classroom. "Only combs show their teeth in public," Father once said, preaching decorum. I ignored the sermon. Now I worried that after I left teaching smiles would melt from the hours, chilling my heart and freezing my face into propriety. "In my dormitory I keep a stuffed cat on the table by my bed," Kirsten told me this semester. "I've attached a fishing line to its tail. Just outside the window of my room is a tall tree with lots of branches. I live in a quadrangle through which campus guides lead prospective students and their parents. Sometimes when I see a group approaching, I toss the cat into the tree then duck below my window sill and meow. Often the groups stop, and I hear people saying things like 'look at that poor cat' and 'oh, dear, what can we do?'" "College is such fun," Kirsten continued. "I'm a junior and have one more year. This summer I am going to practice animal sounds, and next fall when I return, I'll bring more creatures back with me, maybe a flamingo and a monkey and a big green tree frog. My little sister has a stuffed toucan. It is red and blue and easy to see from the ground. I will probably bring it, too."

In February Noelle wrote an essay on money. Her research was sensible and consisted of exploring the campus. At the mini-mart in the student bookstore, a Coca Cola cost $1.00. "Then a little way down the road in the student union convenience store, it costs $1.39, the price of a five minute stroll thirty-nine cents." "If I walk down the steps in the student union to the Union Street Market," she continued, "the Coca Cola costs $1.25, a half minute on the stairs saving me fourteen cents, but the soda still costing a quarter more than it did at the bookstore."

Once the soda lost its fizz, Noelle launched into her real subject, the cost of athletics. "I see," she wrote, "football and basketball players in the dining hall with their 'life coaches.' These people sit with the players and tell them what classes they need to pass, what classes they need to take, and when their classes meet. I want to know why my money is going into the salary of the life coach of someone who should be able to discover where his classes are taught. I'm assuming that being a good athlete means almost being up to academic speed. These guys get to come here free and play on our teams. Following the money trail from my pocket to the life coach, I'm pretty sure that I'm buying an athlete. It's as if I went to a store and saw one in a window, purchased him, and brought him home. I want to know why that cute quarterback isn't escorting me to class and snuggling with me at night. I paid for him to come here, and I have needs, too."

I am fond of corny octogenarian verse and urge students to rummage the library and unearth old poems. Unlike Vicki who usually leaves the room when the arthritic fit seizes me, students respond with limber enthusiasm, eager to display the results of their research. Last Monday I recited a limerick at the beginning of class. "A man tried to get a pink fuchsia / To grow in St. Petersburg Ruchsia / But always in vain, / Till he cried out in much pain, / 'Will nothing, O fuchsia, induchsia?'" "Wonderful," Merrill exclaimed when I finished, "but how about this gem?" "Our dear little Willie / As fair as a lily; / God for him sent / And so we let him went." The poem was familiar. I'd stumbled across Willie's demise several times in my library years, but never had I read the verse Julienne recited. "Oh! Mournful day / That stole away / Poor Mrs. Bly, / Who chanced to die / Of a sky— / Rocket / In her eye— / Socket."

"Joy and Sorrow, twins were born / On a sunny showery April morn." Many years ago I found the couplet in a dusty book and noted it, suspecting time would increase its appeal. At least I believe that now. But, of course, as Charles Pearson stated in 1896 and I jotted down, "No man writes or can write the full truth about himself or other men, because no man thoroughly knows himself or his neighbors." What is certain, however, is that life appears very different at dusky retirement than it does at hot supple noon. No longer do I have stamina enough to brush aside grabby bottom limbs and climb the higher branches of learning. Apophthegmatic sayings and lower, more earthy, regions satisfy me. By the by, a simple *f* transforms *lower* into the appealingly aesthetic *flower*. Indeed as odd crankings grind through my ears and my kidneys flutter strangely, I may be experiencing the second coming of childhood, not an occurrence that awakens the worms of discontent, however, these last, incidentally, easily scotched by Zenoleum, especially in hogs, a factual tidbit I found and made a note of a decade ago.

Grammar was once the scourge of classrooms. Now spoken rules have become unspoken and forgotten. As a result the English I hear often seems a foreign language. "Because they are usually made from wood," as a textbook ought to put it, "doors are generally subjunctive." Certainly grammarians have long debated matters that don't seem important, for example, whether mumps and measles are singular or plural. Their bodily manifestations are obviously singular, but appearances deceive, especially where rhetoric is concerned. In any case words have dimmed and now are rarely beacons of light. Instead they are playthings, the stuffed kittens and toucans of story. "How lucky you are!" the guidance counselor exclaimed addressing a hopeless stutterer, "you were born to be an auctioneer." "I am afraid," Doctor Sollows said to Ada McClarin, "that you suffer from an excess of adipose tissue." "Upon my word, good gracious me," Ada responded, her fingers tapping nervously across her purse, "do you suppose that's the reason I'm so fat?"

Oddly, shattering conventional usage does not necessarily undermine comprehension. Outside the fold of proper grammar and beyond the reach of the good verbal shepherd, his staff crooked into thou-shall-not, words often kick up sounds and frolic into communication. One night last week, when Vicki crept into bed after midnight, I bellowed scoldingly, "Um kateece." Immediately Vicki responded, saying, "Crak pohoe palmagoon," my first "word" rhyming with *hum*, her last with *loon*. For the next four minutes, we repeated our "words" in happy companionship, raising and lowering the syllables, inserting an *f* and other consonants into the scale and making the sounds flower.

"It is impossible," Jerome K. Jerome declared, "to enjoy idling thoroughly unless one has plenty of work to do." Weaving words into ringlets can fill a vacant moment, but it cannot occupy a day, and I worry that after retirement I won't have work enough to keep me busy. As the old saw puts it, fleas only bother the dog in the kennel; the dog on the hunt doesn't scratch. I've grown so accustomed to teaching that wordy doings outside class often irk me. Last Sunday morning Vicki and I went to "That Breakfast Place" in Willimantic. I ate the "Senior Eggs Benedict." My sunny side was up, and I felt spiffy until I asked for an order of "especially crisp" bacon, and the waitress said, "No problem." Later, she said, "Have a nice day" when she handed me the check. "Have a good one," the woman running the cash register said after I paid the bill. Such pleasant pellets make me pass verbs warm as gravel, and I banish them from the schoolhouse. After breakfast Vicki drove to Home Depot, saying

I might find an item inside to occupy me during retirement. I'd never been to Home Depot and was horrified. I am used to shops, not airplane hangars. Moreover, I am not and never will be a tool-using animal. "Why," I almost said to Vicki as we left, "did God create woman if not to hammer and paste?" "Tiger hunting is a fine amusement until the tiger decides to hunt us," I thought, keeping quiet as we left the store, remembering practical wisdom I noted down years ago.

I wonder if the corporate will interest me more after I retire. Commercial doodling has long attracted me, especially that hallowed by age. In May while sauntering the pages of a nineteenth century periodical, I perused columns hawking a box store of items: Garmore's Artificial Ear Drums, offering "Hope for the Deaf" without being "observable," the "infallible" Isbell Mole Trap priced at $2.00, and Wilbor's Compound of Pure Cod-Liver Oil and Lime "for consumptives." The "Shoeopodist" promised to straighten hammer toes and warm frosted feet. Selling for 10 cents for one, six for 25 cents or fifteen for 50 cents, the Swiss Warbler or Mocking-Bird Whistle seemed just the thing for Kirsten "to study" this summer because "after a little practice your mouth will be seem to be a complete menagerie." While The Honorable A. H. Stevens, M. C., and "hundreds of others" thought the Invalid Rolling Chair "a priceless boon to those who are unable to walk," Ayer's Cathartic Pills cured chronic constipation. "the national curse of Americans." "Farewell Swamp Root and Lily Dear," I thought, closing the magazine and hoping Vicki would never be forced to purchase a rolling chair for me. But if she did, I thought, I want a scooter—a speedy one without a governor. "One with squirrel tails on the handlebars," I said aloud, "long ones like those I tied on the handlebars of my bicycle with fishing line when I was a boy."

Sometimes I think that in retirement all my tomorrows will be todays. Of course I'll continue doing things that occupy me now: raking leaves, shoveling snow, picking up sticks, and mowing grass. I will probably rub the dogs more. Unfortunately Suzy and Jack are less responsive than they once were. They're approaching middle age. They haven't begun pulling trousers up to their breast bones in order to hide the incipient swelling of midriffs, but they are aging and sleeping more than in the past. Even contemplating retirement has changed some aspects of life. I live more in my dreams although I don't play a leading role in them. Recently I dreamed that a vast colony of social wasps invaded the earth. Silver and three feet in length, the wasps looked like small military drones. They hunted humans for food and were immune to pesticides. For a while people tried to kill them by using long swords and slicing through their exoskeletons. When this method failed to eradicate large numbers of wasps, groups of people fled into caves and attempted to live out of sight, sallying forth only to harvest food, dressed in white hazmat suits.

Individual wasp stings were painful but not fatal unless a person was simultaneously stung three or more times. What complicated matters was the fact that if a wasp bit rather than stung a living person that person's DNA entered the wasp's body and became part of the wasp's genetic composition. The bite itself served as a kind of vaccination, preventing the person's DNA from being passed to any other wasps, no matter the number of times he was bitten. The result was that although the insects' physical bodies—head, mesosoma, and metasoma— remained wasp-like, their inner natures changed, causing wasps to behave like the humans they bit. In the dream I did not live years enough in evolutionary time to witness the long-term effects of the transformation. I was pessimistic, however, when I awoke, thinking man's DNA would cause the wasps to regress into irrationality and anti-social individualism. As for the cave-dwellers, they vanished. Either the wasps swatted them out of existence or they drilled cells deep underground, eventually turning white and coming to resemble termites more than people, feeding on the roots of trees.

Joy's twin Sorrow eventually produces children of her own, Anxiety and Concern, the latter usually focusing on others and involving medical matters. Instead of planning the intellectual, I suspect I will spend much of my retirement discussing the physical, most of the conversation dark but a little smacking of the bitter-sweetly humorous. So many of my male friends have suffered from collapsed drainage pipes that a plaque with their names chiseled on it should be placed inside the urology department at Windham Hospital. One of my buddies has even framed a catheter and hung it in his study beside his diplomas. "B. A., M. A., Ph. D. and M. D. (Medical Device)," my friend Josh said, "marking the wayfaring male academic's progress toward the Celestial City."

Yesterday I walked for two hours. Tiles of ice shingled the Fenton River. The wind was strong, turning trees into whisks sweeping back and forth. Branches snapped and fell, skittering across the icy glaze covering the snow. Sparrows rode the bucketing air clinging to the canes of multiflora rose. A turkey vulture planed through wind shears and flew through a window opening into a hay loft. I followed deer trails. Several times I was careless and stepped off the beaten track. My weight broke the hard surface of the snow, and one of my legs sank to the ground two feet below. Righting myself was difficult. I leaned forward on my forearms and levered my leg up and out. Twice my arms sank, and I fell on my chest, chin spading into the snow. By the end of the walk my fingers and toes ached. The cold, though, quickened my feelings, and I knew that so long as I didn't sink immobile into ailments I'd spend many retirement hours outside. Encounters with the actual are merciful. They keep life busy and bestow forgetfulness. A punning old saw states that the man who looks spruce in old age does not pine for youth. The truth may actually be that the person who looks into spruce pines for little. The sight of small birds light on the wing can raise heavy spirits.

    Adjusting to retirement may be easy because I have long avoided the intense. I have never been a fan. I haven't experienced deep passion. Neither fervor nor belief has ridden me like a hobby-horse. Intensity constricts, and because my commitments are weak and temporary, I have remained flexible. I'm capable of altering direction and shedding interests, accommodating myself to the changing conditions of life. I run half-marathons. Because I am a poor athlete and have always been a terrible runner, where I finish does not matter. No personal standard of excellence exists against which my times can be measured, producing melancholy, as it does in friends who once ran well and swiftly, in fact narrowing their living, leading them to give up running races. When found, I'll make notes of things, enjoying them for themselves and not pondering their significance. Last summer, the president of a northern college said, "Much may be done with a Canadian if he is caught young." Recently a television preacher broadcasting from Birmingham declared, "Only the mercy of God prevented the prodigal son from taking a pistol and blowing his brains out." Many of my notes refer to suspect tales. Two years ago, the *Chattanooga Times Free Press* published an article entitled "Aging with Dignity." For the piece a free-lance writer reported interviewing Deuteronomy Chettle, a farmer in Decherd, Tennessee. Deuteronomy was ninety-six years old. He still planted tobacco and drove a tractor. He had also outlived two wives. His present wife had "the bad sugar" and was confined to a wheelchair. "Her suitcase is packed, and soon she'll be boarding with the Lord. She'll get new teeth and be able to eat desserts again," Deuteronomy confided. "When I married her, I expected that she'd wrap crape around my box, but I'm feeling lively right now, particularly lively, and I reckon it will take another one or two wives to see me through." On a lighter but just as "divine" a note, Stephanie read a wondrously absurd poem in class on Thursday. "Oh, the corn, the horrible corn, / Burning at night, aching at morn. / Under somebody's foot half of the time / Throbbing with misery, almost sublime. / Paining, / Inflaming. / Big as your fist. / Show me the sign of the / Po-di-a-trist!"

Calm

"What are you thinking about?" Vicki said as I sat at the kitchen table. "An essay on calm," I answered. "Well," Vicki said, "there is never much of that around me." In the middle of the table sat a tub of peanut butter. Taped to the side of the tub was a yellow post-it. Printed on it in black letters, both words underlined three times, was, "Sam-No!" Stuck to the lid of the tub was another post-it. Written on it was, "Sam, this is not for you! If you keep eating peanut butter, you will be TOO FAT for your clothes, for your road races, and for the cruise in December. I will not go on a cruise with a FAT MAN. The time for action is NOW!" Two nights later during dessert, Vicki exploded into criticism of males, the bad behavior of the head of the International Monetary Fund and the former governor of California catalysts. "But," I said, "Not all men are bad. My name ought to be Goody Two-Shoes. We have been married for 32 years, and..." Vicki did not let me finish. "Be quiet," she shouted. "Besides you are not a type A personality. With those soft brown eyes, you aren't even type C."

Self-medication is not for youth. Recently I read about a young man so bedeviled by deer flies that he shaved his head after which he had a swatter tattooed across the top. In contrast years of satisfactory marital life have taught me sound, almost infallible, medical procedure. When Vicki suddenly becomes stormy, I decamp for the university library. There I dose myself with pharmaceutical reading. I do not immerse myself in the literature of benzodiazepines. Instead I peruse notices for patent medicines. Reading shapes mood. After a column of ads, peace of mind returns, and life seems a tub of peanut butter, glistening, inviting, almost imploring me to jab my index finger inside and scoop out a crunchy, wondrously fattening mouthful. The boy who relied on ink to combat deer flies would have done better to put his trust in Tough on Flies, "the only reliable lotion positively preventing Flies, Gnats and Insects of every description from annoying Horses and Cattle." At the end of the nineteenth century a gallon can cost only $1.50, and if cut with, say, buttermilk, probably worked as well on bipeds as it did on quadrupeds. Still, if the flyblown had reservations about Tough on Flies, they could have purchased Bug Death, which despite containing "no arsenic" killed "potato, squash, and cucumber bugs, currant and tomato worms, green fly or louse on rose bushes."

I pop out of bed at five in the morning. Vicki sleeps until eight or nine. One day last week, however, I discovered Vicki in the kitchen at seven-thirty. "Oh," I said, "Seeing you this early surprises me. I didn't hear you say 'good morning.'" "I didn't say 'good morning,'" Vicki replied leaning over the sink, "I had pressing needs in the pantry." "Okay," I said, and thinking the day's domestic weather might be unsettled, I set out for the library. In a library, home is where memories lurk. When I was a boy, I spent summers on my grandfather's dairy farm in Virginia, and advertisements for matters rural are sedatives. "When a cow forgets to breed," I read in *The New-England Homestead*, "it is no sign that she is ready to die—but a symptom of something wrong which Injecto Vaginae will cure." "Lots of eggs" were the result of feeding hens green cut bone, a notice for Mann's Green Bone Cutter declared.

Many advertisements publicized elixirs guaranteed to heal the bruised and invigorate the listless. "Home is the keystone of a woman's life," a testimonial for Dr. Pierce's Favorite Prescription stated. "Any weakness or disease which incapacitates her so she cannot fulfill the exalted function of motherhood is the saddest blight that can come upon a woman's life." The favorite prescription banished cankers and anthracnoses from women's lives turning their days green and fertile, giving "healthy power and capacity to the special organs" and by reinforcing "the nerve-centers" made "natural motherhood possible, safe and comparatively easy." "Women do not like to tell a Doctor the details of their private ills," another advertisement noted, not even pharmacologists as skilled as Dr. Pierce. As a result countless women suffered "in silence from multiple disorders connected with their sexual system." These "modest, sensitive" women were urged to consult Lydia Pinkham in Lynn, Massachusetts. Her "advice," the notice assured readers, "is based upon the greatest experience ever possessed by man or woman in this country, and extends over a period of twenty-three years, and thousands upon thousands of cases." "Healthy Old People," an advertisement for Ripans Tabules recounted, "say the main thing to do is to keep the stomach, liver and bowels in order if you want to live long and keep well." While Dr. Greene's Nervura purified the blood and strengthened the nerves and came highly recommended by "Corbett the Mighty," Alkavis, extracted from the "well-known Kava-Kava Shrub" which grew on the banks of the Ganges, cured almost everything, ranging from kidney and bladder diseases, rheumatism and dropsy, to gravel in the back.

Readers of such advertisements must carefully measure dosages of paragraphs. A tablespoon of ailments too many, and one begins to experience sympathetic symptoms. Before anxiety sets in like butt rot, however, remedies are close to the eye. In 1897 the Laughing Camera and its two lenses cost ten cents, just the thing, I thought, to dry mildew and transform worry into good cheer. "You look through the lenses," an advertisement instructed, "and your stout friends will look like living skeletons, your thin friends like dime store museum fat men."

Not everyone is strong enough to tolerate a regimen of advertisements. What oils my hours can cause someone else to break out in hives. Last Monday Harry told me that because of a doctor's appointment he would not be able to run with me on Tuesday. As a result I ran later than I normally do on Tuesday. When I got to the university track, Harry was jogging alone. He explained that he'd mistaken the date of the appointment. "Gee, I hope you haven't been bored," I said. "No," he answered, "I have been thinking about the three worst mistakes of my life." Harry looked simultaneously doleful and agitated. To smooth his mood, I dosed him with home-brewed acetylsalicylic acid, cornpone that lifts the listener out of the labyrinth of the past, making him forget the Minotaur of error, causing him to bleat "Holy Cow." "How old are you?" Vernice Singleton asked Liddy Gruel. "I ain't sure," Liddy answered, "but I know I'm younger than you. What's your earliest memory?" "Well, I remember one thing from the time I was in my cradle," Vernice replied. "I remember hearing two people say as you walked by Ma and Pa's front porch, 'There goes old Liddy Gruel. Look at her, poor soul. She sure is ancient. She's practically a cripple. It's a wonder she can walk.'" Occasionally a single tale does not restore calm, and the good naturopath must double the dosage. This past summer Ada McClarin visited Europe for the first time. On Ada's return, Vernice asked her if she saw the aqueducts when she was in Rome. "Saw them!" Ada exclaimed. "I took pictures of them. They swam beautifully, much better than the ratty old mallards paddling about on the cow ponds here in Smith County."

If story fails to blunt anxiety, one can inject a syringe of puns into conversation, jabbing them in rapid staccato, not giving a listener an opportunity to flinch. Puns surge through the bloodstream. On reaching the brain they anesthetize the nervous system, restoring calm of mind, a glazed expression revealing that the medicine has done its job. A typical syringe might contain a compound composed of synapse inhibitors similar to the following: "A Christian woman cannot change her sex because she would be a he then" and "Angry sheiks are harem-scarem sorts of fellows." Poetry is dangerous and should be injected only when a sufferer is wildly agitated, a time-tested palliative being: "I think of thee, sweet William, / And I long to hear from you. / Send me a missive, won't you please? / Oh, come now, *billet-doux*."

    A person can do several things to gain equilibrium. He should not, however, ponder happiness and certainly not attempt a definition as it changes frequently, a lost circus ticket destroying the joy of a child, a vanished fortune undermining the spirits of an adult. One should live common-sensibly. The blind, for example, should avoid eating peas off knives. Age, of course, is the progenitor of reasonable living as Time wears away the prickings of envy and covetousness. The din of mountebanks pandering dreams and colporteurs hawking guides to eternity becomes silent. Zeal ceases to disturb. Last month I resigned from the local chapter of the Robin Hood Society, finally accepting that my neighbors were immune to sense and would go to their graves damned—unreformed and unrepentant. Such awareness does not, of course, matter. In cities people rarely notice the heavens. Light is artificial and focused downward making parochial doings glow with importance. In the deep country man sees the stars and realizes his world is a speck amid untold specks, an understanding that's an antidote to fretting ambition and vanity.

    Calm eventually becomes habitual. The valley always seems peaceful, and Sweet Afton never floods the "green braes." I don't splatter my pages with the novelist's gore or the poet's lust. I write essays. My advice has never alleviated, or worsened, an injustice. "The essayist knows only too well that nothing he can say will prevent the world from going up in flames. Hence he leaves fires," Robert Lynd wrote, "to other people, the minority of whom try to put them out and the majority of whom heartily enjoy them." After a time, even dreams cease to disrupt. Two weeks ago I dreamed that Vicki and I had agreed to fly across Connecticut with a stunt pilot. The pilot's plane was a yellow by-wing. Just as the man was strapping me into my seat, I changed my mind, thinking, "This is crazy." To save us from plummeting to our deaths, I forced myself to wake before the plane left the ground. After I aborted the take-off, I sat up and looked around. "A close call," I said before falling back asleep and spending the rest of the night at a low, sensible altitude.

Even meticulous planning cannot strip inconsistency from life, however. No matter how a man bolts his food, eventually the nuts won't hold. For me an extended period of calm resembles a smothering heat wave, and after time I long for an invigorating change in my internal weather. Consequently a summons for jury duty in Rockville raised my spirits, especially since I was called to the Criminal Court. Forty-three people were summoned. Immediately four were excused. One was deaf while another expected to give birth within the week. Of the thirty-nine remaining potential jurors, I was the first interviewed by the judge, prosecutor, and defense. Before being interviewed all of us watched an instructive film, teaching such things as "The law does not allow a case to be decided on the basis of sympathy" and "Jurors may not start their own investigation of the case."

My interview took nineteen minutes. During the interview I was asked simple questions, among others, if I was married and how many children I had. When asked if I would give more credence to the word of a policeman than to a career criminal, I said, "Certainly," after which the judge noted that in a trial all testimony had to be weighed the same. The defense lawyer asked me to study the defendant and tell the court what he looked like. "Just a young guy," I said, silently thinking, however, that no one could look more like a blackguard. On being asked if I had ever experienced trouble with the police, I felt embarrassed, answering that my life had been so placid that I had never been stopped for speeding or even received a parking ticket. When the prosecutor asked if I would apply the law as the judge instructed, I replied that in the jury room I was the judge. I said that I would ignore any instructions I thought led to injustice. I then cited the Jim Crow laws of my childhood in Tennessee, saying legality and morality were not always the same, "a lesson no American should and no Southerner can forget." "Professor," the judge said, "that's true, but this is just a burglary case." After sixteen minutes of deliberation, I was excused from the jury. "Professor," the judge said, "I'm sorry you won't be on the jury, but I am going to read a couple of your books." "So am I," said the prosecutor.

"When does the case start?" Vicki said when I returned home. "It doesn't start for me," I answered. "I was excused from the jury." "Does that mean you will be around the house getting in my way all week?" Vicki said. "No," I answered, "I'll be spending many hours in the library." "Reading advertisements again?" Vicki asked. "No," I replied, "this time I am going to read letters country children wrote to magazines in the nineteenth century describing their lives." The letters were stronger pacifiers than the advertisements as children almost always described their pets. "I have a dog. His name is King," Tommy wrote. "He eats corn, potatoes, tomatoes, apples, chestnuts, cherries, beans, candy, grapes, and oranges." "My sister Maud just died. She was eighteen years old," Alice recounted. "She taught Old Gray our cat how to open a door and shake hands. Old Gray sleeps a lot. I think he misses Maud." "I plowed and dragged for my father while he was away threshing," Ned

The Splendour Falls

related. "I had three rabbits and the dog killed one of them and a mink killed the other, and the other one died. I had four crows and three of them died. I have one of them yet. His name is Blackie and he can talk pretty well. Mama had about 70 chickens, but the rats killed and ate all but four of them. One of our neighbors lost a two-year old heifer over the bluff. It fell about 200 feet and broke its neck." "I am six years old," Gertrude wrote. "I have a little white Kitty named Snowball. When I stoop over to get anything, she will jump on my back. I lived in Texas for three years and in Ohio for three years. Papa calls me his little Texas girl, and my little brother his Buckeye. I had a bed in the garden and Papa bought all my vegetables. Little brother had 10 onions and a beet and a sunflower in his bed."

After a week of letters my blood pressure sank so dangerously that my arteries were on the verge of collapse. Not even ludicrous statements could pump them back up, embalmed remarks like, "If flesh is grass as the Bible states, then a lot of folks are loads of hay." I needed additional self-medication, this to stimulate rather than calm. At the end of the month I read at the Connecticut Book Festival in Hartford. In hopes of inducing life-enhancing hypertension into the day, I began my presentation, saying, "I want to take advantage of this grand occasion to announce that as of now I am a candidate for the Republican nomination for the presidency of these great United States. Unlike the sorry peckerwoods who have announced previously, I am extraordinarily humble and stunningly intelligent. Moreover I have cogitated long on political matters. You may ask me if President Obama was born in this red, white, and blue nation. I answer, 'Certainly not. He was born in Hawaii—a foreign country, one of those palm-tree islands cruise ships visit, not a mainline American shotgun-and-copperhead-front-porch-guzzle-your-moonshine-out-of-Tupperware place.' Even worse, he can't accomplish anything. I'm not saying he's lazy, but he is the sort of fellow who takes a nap before he goes to sleep." When shock and awe, wild huzzahs, and the uncontrolled stamping of feet did not greet my declaration, I forged on, saying that my next public appearance would be at the Iron Horse Half-Marathon in Simsbury on June 5. "I will be at the back of the peloton, chatting with aged widows in hopes of raising money for my campaign."

"How did the audience react to the announcement?" Vicki asked when I returned home. "A girl smiled, and two men looked puzzled," I said; "that's it." "The next time," Vicki said, "don't tear the new leaf when you turn it over." "Right," I said, "How's this: 'A widow is like a garden run wild. Cultivate her, and her weeds will disappear.'" The horticultural references budded over night, and the next morning I wandered the end of May. The wanderer's mind see-saws wondrously, one moment floating up into stimulation the next drifting down into comfortable, satisfactory calm. Hundreds of wild yellow iris bloomed along the creek in the low damp of Valentine Meadow. Water yawled around coppery elbows of the Fenton River. A pair of Canada geese steered three goslings into a bind of snags. The goslings' down was furry as an old army blanket, first brown then gold in the dappled light. A hen turkey hunkered low near the river and spread her wings into a tent to shelter her chicks. Beside wet briary thickets cow parsnip rose in heavy knobs. Buds on laurel had swollen into muffins. Blossoms dangled from black locust, from a distance looking like necklaces of cowry shells. Orioles slipped in and through gray dogwood almost as if they were playing hide and seek, their orange and black feathers carnival masks. While stamens curved long and lush from pink azalea, the short tufts of those on arrow wood hovered over flats of petals in a yellow haze. A young black racer oozed through a low mound of stones, its scales shining like newly cut facets. A red squirrel shimmied up a white pine.

A glaze of pollen covered the beaver pond, and royal fern grew thick as privet, its leaves spreading in broken green droplets. Bullet galls splattered scrub oaks, and fragrant bedstraw transformed a sandy trail into a dressing room. A Hereford bull lounged in a shady pasture, his head rising above the grass like a lumpy boulder white and rough with lichens. Wood frogs sprang from the musty anonymity of last year's leaves; young chipmunks left the safety of stone-wall burrows and scampered about recklessly, and an osprey dove into Mirror Lake, tacking away from then reversing and flying through a squall of red-winged blackbirds.

Turtles were laying eggs. I removed two wood turtles from the center of a dirt road. I placed them beyond the shoulder in rumpled gravel, good spots in which to dig and to deposit eggs. As I drove home along Route 195, I saw a snapping turtle approaching the asphalt. Traffic ran in killing chains, so I pulled into a bus stop. The turtle was heavy and bigger than the round pointed blade of a shovel. I forced the turtle into the dog cage Vicki keeps in the car after which I drove to a nearby pond, located in the direction in which turtle was headed but which lay beyond the state highway, a local road, and the entrance to a busy parking lot. When I freed the turtle, it snapped at me then shuffled into the pond, disappearing under a cloud of muddy water. Nearby a fringe tree ballooned into shreds, the plumy white blossoms almost sweeping me off the ground. "How was the roaming?" Vicki asked when I got home. "Super," I said, "wood and field were green and brimming with life." "That's good," Vicki said. "While you were gone, I made rice pudding, covered with cinnamon and filled with raisins just as you like it." "Oh, boy," I said, thinking that maybe I wouldn't be going to the library after dinner.

My Secret Life

I don't have a secret life. I've never had a secret life. My books are bigger than my life. I cannot explain why I missed having a secret life. Perfection and dry conventionality bore me, and I think mendacity a particularly appealing form of wit. Moreover I'm energetic and have a good appetite. Last Sunday morning I ran eight miles. At the end of the run I almost felt middle-aged again, and for breakfast I grazed across a corpuscular landscape of eggs, bacon, toast, and home fries, these last an oil patch crusty with burned grease and bilious with charred onions and green peppers. Despite describing my doings in two shelves of books, I have not exposed myself. Intellectual nudity repulses me. Never have I revealed that my favorite food is peanut butter, a gustatory confession sure to titillate readers into exclaiming, "My word" while pressing fingertips fluttering to their lips in astonishment.

Although I don't have a secret life, I usually keep rancorous feelings private, smothering them under the cold cream of manners. One morning during a cruise last year, Vicki and I toured the botanical garden on St. Vincent's. We arrived at the garden at the same time as four other passengers from the boat, two women from Vancouver and a couple from Belfast. At the entrance, guides herded tourists into groups. The charge for the tour was five dollars a person, the guides pocketing all tips. The guide who escorted us knew plants and talked so well and enthusiastically that delight blossomed across the morning. The tour lasted an hour and a half. At the end I tipped the guide twenty dollars. The Canadians and the Irish gave him nothing. Instead they turned their backs on him and hurried out of the garden. "Damn such niggardliness," Vicki said, "the guides don't have a pot to piss in. In comparison people like us have everything." "To hell with those bastards," I said and handed the guide another twenty dollars. "Thank you," he said, "I really thank you." "Ten dollars to tour the garden and a forty dollar tip," Vicki said, "and worth every cent." During the remainder of the cruise I met our garden companions several times. Sight of them repulsed me. I remained silent, however, nodding and smiling, keeping my acidic feelings secret.

I inhabit daylight. I eavesdrop, but I don't do it surreptitiously. I carry a pencil and pad openly. Last week I jotted down a conversation between two women sitting in the waiting room of the Windham Eye Group in Willimantic. "I'm not ready for fall. This summer went too fast," a woman in a gray dress said. "Much too fast," a woman sitting across from her answered, her head bobbing up and down like a pendulum on its side. "Yes, much too fast, much too fast," the first woman responded, turning herself into an old-fashioned repeater. Occasionally conversation is livelier. Last Monday Eliza got engaged to her college boyfriend, Travis. They drove down to Connecticut from Massachusetts to tell Vicki and me. Vicki celebrated by baking a chocolate cake and making tomato and eggplant soup. Before eating we jumped into a magnum of champagne and cannonaded about. Eliza and Travis started dating when they were sophomores. "What a long life you'll have together," Vicki said. "Yes," Travis replied, "Forty-five years from now, we'll be seventy. We won't know who or where we are. We will have lost our teeth and be in wheelchairs, but we'll be together." "You insensitive bastard," I said. "I will be seventy in two weeks." "Oh, Daddy," Eliza simpered. "You don't look seventy. None of my friends think you are that old." Often I repeat the words of others, never anything mystifying, however. Readers know that I have a tooth for verbal sweets, and they send me nougats for the page. "Enclosed is a scrumptious pun I found in June," a man wrote from South Carolina. "I lost it on my desk for three months, but despite the heat, it didn't melt." "Why are bee hives like potatoes covered in smut?" my correspondent asked. "Because," he answered, "the first are bee holders and the second specked taters."

The memory is a mausoleum of the forgotten, in effect secrets because they have vanished from consciousness and have not been shared with others. Recently a childhood friend wrote, addressing me as "Pick," a nickname that slipped from me after eighth grade. "Daddy, you are not Pick," Eliza said. "Not now," I said, "certainly not now, but maybe I was Pick sixty years ago." A failing memory, of course, transforms most of the past into permanent secrets. On Tuesday, I couldn't recall Joan Baez's name. "The skinny balladeer with long black hair, Bob Dylan's friend, one of the anti-war voices during the Viet-Nam era," I said in class. "Many of her songs were seductively melancholy. Her rendition of 'We Shall Overcome' became a Civil Rights Anthem. Years later, John Didion described her harshly in *Slouching Toward Bethlehem*. All of you know her name." Of course the class could not identify her, and when I eventually unlocked Time's vault and retrieved the name, not a single student had heard of her. Even more startling was the fact that no student could recite the nursery rhyme, "Aphrodite without her nightie." Oddly as memory rusts and I lose keys to my past, I shore up the present with shards from strangers' lives. Four days ago at a tag sale on Mansfield City Road, I paid fifty cents for a cracked white plate. The plate was six inches in diameter. Printed around the rim in black letters was "Souvenir. East Greenwich, R. I." In the bowl of the plate a brown cat crouched, lapping milk from a blue dish. Tied around the cat's neck was a gold bow while a wreath of violets circled the milk dish.

I cannot explain buying the plate. When I saw the plate, however, recollection of an afternoon in Nova Scotia popped unaccountably out of the past into the present. One bright day in July Vicki and I drove to Bear River. We bought four quarts of local cherries, small, tart, and addictive. While Vicki looked at shawls in a knitting shop, I sat on a boulder, ate cherries, and talked to a Mi'qmak woman. The woman gave me a present, braiding a bracelet out of deer hide. "You are now a member of the deer tribe," she said, tightening the bracelet around my wrist. Afterward she picked up a drum and played a "healing" tune for me. I don't know what the woman noticed that provoked the tune. I thought I looked dandy, and without a secret life what meets the eye is all there is. Two evenings later, Vicki and I went to Yarmouth and saw the movie *Cowboys and Aliens*. The night was foggy and dark, and I drove back to Beaver River slowly. Suddenly near Port Maitland the horizon burst into light. Across the highway and one hundred and fifty yards west of Four Winds, our home, a house exploded in flames, the fire billowing and breaking over the road, tossing ash like waves pitching suds above high tide.

The blaze had been set, and for days brush fires of rumors scorched the neighborhood. The next morning I walked along the road to the house. An acidic mist hung over the ruins. One chimney remained standing while a second looked like a broken canine. Walls had vanished and collapsed black and smoldering. An iron stove lay beached on its side, and here and there beams jutted from the ashes shrunken and ribbed by flames. Six jowly, hamburgerish men stood near the wreckage, all in Wellingtons, and one in a jump suit with "Fire Marshal" on the back in yellow letters. Two days later a volunteer fireman told me that getting away with burning one's house down was easy. "The best way to start the fire," he said, "is to place a toaster on a table in the kitchen. Stuff the toaster with kindling rather than bread. Make sure that the kindling is tall enough to reach a curtain. Switch the toaster on and leave the house." "Three years ago," the man continued, "a fellow in our town burned his house down this way. He was an avid hunter, and guns were the love of his life. He removed all eight of his guns before starting the fire. We found them in the trunk of his car."

I hadn't suppressed recollections of Nova Scotia. Like water coursing through a creek in the spring, the day had spooled out over the lowland of summer and sunk traceless into earthy memory, only to be spaded up and tapped by the dish through an inexplicable process of association. Suppression, however, often quickens, and many secrets endure only because they are suppressed. Some years ago bumper stickers celebrating the familial rather than advocating the political were remarkably faddish, especially in Fairfield County. The most popular sticker read "Proud Parent of an Honors Student." One fall a sociologist at Yale decided to study the prevalence of the sticker. For two weeks she used roadside cameras to photograph the backs of cars traveling four roads in Greenwich: Round Hill Road, Lake Avenue, Old Mill, and Clapboard Ridge Road. She programmed the cameras to ignore vehicles with out of state license plates. The cameras also deleted repeat appearances of individual cars, thus preventing errand-running local residents from skewing the statistics.

The results were frightening. 28.2% of the automobiles on the four roads were, in sociological terms, "carriers," the sticker prominent on bumpers or trunks. "In a locale in which divorce rates are higher than in any other county in Connecticut, indeed among the highest in affluent areas of the United States, and kept from ascending even higher by the fabulous cost of divorce, the incidence of domestic sloganeering reveals the prevalence of a potentially socially disruptive displacement." "As their marriages threaten to shatter, parents," the study continued, "behave in a compensatory manner. Instead of solving their problems, they shift attention on to their children. As their own dreams of happiness fade, parents become inordinately ambitious for their children. Under the cloak of pride and of promoting education, they destroy adolescence, transforming their offspring into the bearers of broken hopes. They burden youth with expectations children are ill-equipped to carry." "If this trend continues and grows," the study concluded, "it will likely create another 'lost generation,' youngsters crippled by the weight of their parents' problems and as a result susceptible to anti-social temptations associated in the vernacular with tuning or opting out." Results of the study never appeared in print although according to hearsay, it was much talked about at the Round Hill and Greenwich Country clubs. A "village" of politicians, educators, bankers, and promoters of many affluent stripes, especially realtors, combined and urged Yale to suppress the study "for the greater community good." As a result the sociologist unexpectedly won an intramural grant, enabling her to spend a year in Papua New Guinea studying the "symbolic and actual use" of Bird of Paradise feathers in ceremonial headdresses. Her earlier study, however, remains a secret that Time has not quite shushed into nothingness.

Vicki says I'm a "fantadler" skipping from one interest to another. "You spiff around too quickly to have secrets." I went for a walk yesterday afternoon. Quivers of arrowhead bloomed in the muck surrounding Mirror Lake. The shoulders of the dirt road running through the Beaver Meadow were yellow and bushy with goldenrod and small white daisies. No, I am not a "fantadler" or even Pick. If I'm occasionally other than myself, I am a flower. Perhaps I'm a rambling rose, a Dorothy Perkins, the canes of which slide out and across other plants transforming them into trellises. The flowers are scentless, but they blossom in ruffled pink bouquets. From a distance they cheer the weary eye. They make the lacquered surface of life seem sufficient unto the years and cause people to smile, turning moments almost lyrical.

Yesterday just thinking about rambling roses cheered me and somehow brought to mind a happy obituary, "Here lies the body of W. W. / Who never more will trouble you, trouble you."

Ignorance is a type of secret, the dispelling of which does not always delight. For years I imagined, nay, assumed, that the Zinnia was named for a Greek maiden, a lovely childlike woman whose hair spilled over her forehead in wondrously colored locks. My Zinnia lived in bucolic obscurity and golden peace somewhere near the source of the Illissus River, perhaps amid sacred cypress on a bank above a holy spring, a sanctuary where animals came to drink, their blood quarrels momentarily forgotten. Zinnia lived in virginal joy until one day goatish Pan saw her bathing in the honeyed waters of the spring. He dug his hoofs into the ground and galloped after her, splashing through the spring, his lust boiling and polluting the water like rust. Zinnia fled before him like a breeze, delicate and, alas, too weak to outrun his riotous, stormy nature. Artemis happened to be in the wood, however. She took pity on the girl, and just as Pan reached out to seize and savage Zinnia, Artemis shot her with an enchanted arrow, turning her into a flower, one that appeals to innocence, to children and grandparents, one of its vernacular names being "youth and old age." Unfortunately I learned recently that the provenance of Zinnia was far less romantic. The flower was named for Johann Gottfried Zinn, a German botanist. Zinn discovered the flower in Mexico early in the eighteenth century.

Only on the page do I glimpse dark halls and shadowy nooks. Real secrets would lumber me with complexity, not a weight I am inclined to lift. In truth I rarely bark my mind against paragraphs bumpy with secrets. During university terms I read more student papers than books. Students are optimistic, and their writings are congenial, celebrating surfaces rather than mulling secrets into indigestible pessimism. "I am convinced by

C. S. Lewis's moral law, Aristotle's theory on motion, and by my mother's dinner table conversation that there is a God," Fred wrote. Before my eight o'clock lecture on Thursday, I received an e-mail from John. "I woke up this morning feeling a strong compulsion to stay home and not go to class. I do not know the reason for this, but I have learned it is always wise to pay attention to such impulses. I will be absent today for this reason." "Quite right," I answered, adding, "I am sure you are aware that an eclipse gives the sun time for reflection. On the other hand did you know that dead people are the primary cause of earthquakes? Moldering eventually becomes boring. Waiting for the Resurrection exasperates John R. Corpse, and like fans after an international soccer game, the basketed riot, shaking the taproots of trees and tossing boulders through underground caverns." Of course, according to old tales, some people bypass the Resurrection and take The Sunrise Special directly through the clouds. In 1881, William Mathews recounted that Godfrey Kneller, the English portrait painter, dreamed about ascending to Glory as he lay on his deathbed. On returning to consciousness Kneller reported that his name produced a commotion among the princes and potentates gathered about the Gate to Heaven. "As I approached, St. Peter very civilly asked my name. I said it was Kneller. I had no sooner said so than Saint Luke, who was standing just by, turned toward me and said, with a great deal of sweetness, 'What! The famous Sir Godfrey Kneller of England?' 'The very same, sir,' says I, 'at your service.'"

Aside from being genetically disposed to superficiality, not until last Thursday was I able to explain why I've never had a secret life. "Most of the time we do not think about balance," Caitlin stated in an essay. "The central pattern generator in the spinal cord allows us to walk rhythmically without input from the brain, and the semicircular canals and otoliths in the inner ear keep us upright and focused. I only think of balance when it is lacking, and, as such, is annoying. I cannot tolerate a stone in one shoe or carrying too many books in one arm. When I was younger every time I was given a high five, I hit my thigh with the other hand so that my palms stung equally. Most people I have asked say that they did the same thing. They cannot tolerate unequal sensations on opposite sides of the body. If they turn their heads to the right, they quickly rotate them to the left." For my part I have almost no physical balance. I totter when I walk. I don't dance; I stagger. For me all flat surfaces are washed-out and potholed. I can trip without moving my feet. I maintain equilibrium, however, not by slapping a leg or turning my head. I counter the physical imbalance of my body by being overly rational and commonsensical. Because my body wobbles, my mind moves at a preternaturally steady gait. A secret life would break that pace. Such a disruption will not occur, however. A person becomes his habits, and I am too old a courser to change mental stride. Of course this makes me dull. Happily students keep my days lively and intriguing. "People are too hopeful," Alice wrote in her last paper. "They come into the coffee shop where I work at six in the morning grinding their teeth. I can only imagine that the high hopes they had for the day have already been crushed. This is inspiring. I do not have as much hope in a year as some people lose within an hour of waking up." Alice needed cheering, and in the margin of her paper, I wrote, "A pig pen is made to hold pigs. A pig pen may exist when there are no pigs, but pigs are absolutely necessary for the existence of a pen of pigs." "Where did you stumble across that chitterling?" Vicki asked after I read my comment to her. "Ah," I answered, "that's my secret."

Not All There

I didn't expect to teach this fall. I planned to be elsewhere. I intended to retire, but an agreement between university employees and the state of Connecticut hit an Internal Revenue Service speed bump. My intentions vanished into a bureaucratic mist, and so at the beginning of September I was in the classroom. "It's part of the social contract," Stephen Dunn wrote in *Different Hours*, "to seem to be where your body is." I'm a polished actor. Every morning at eight, my body is in class, pacing the boards. My mind, however, is often elsewhere. I spent much of a class period last week on my knees in the field behind our barn in Nova Scotia picking low bush blueberries. Outside the classroom window in Storrs, thunder bellowed, and the sky was dark as asphalt. In Canada the sky was blue and clear, and the day was sunny. I heard a hawk "screal" and later watched a flock of cedar waxwings settle into spruce at the edge of the field, the birds turning about, looking like weathervanes.

Near the end of class I drove Highway 101 toward Yarmouth. Dead porcupines lay clumped along the shoulders of the road, blood black and dry underneath, their loafy bodies battered into fists, here and there crows picking at crusts. In Yarmouth I visited the ox barn at the Southwestern Nova Scotia Exhibition. In the stalls were thirty-four teams of oxen, some standing, others lying down, looking like massive duffel bags, the contents having slipped and shifted toward the end bound by pelvis and tied by tail. As I read the names, Lion and Bright, Spark and Toby, Star and Dan, I listened to the cow bells. Vicki felt sorry for the oxen, saying that the bells probably made them nervous. For my part I heard a carillon ringing after church on Sunday, celebrating the dark earth, its incense rich with sawdust and silage, urine and manure, smoky and dreamy, the fragrance sweeping words away and making me want to roam pastures and use my hands.

Rarely do I observe the room in which I teach: its cinder block walls, linoleum floor, flat fluorescent light, and behind me, cooling boards, broad biers of white blackboard. On Friday I was back in Canada, and I noticed a single stem of New England asters blooming yellow and blue with five blossoms. The stem flourished in a place more improbable than my classroom—in a sleeve of bark silvery and green with lichens and loose around a snaggled stump. On a wide grassy path running between winterberry was a fairy group of thirteen yellow fly agaric mushrooms. Some of the mushrooms had just pushed up through the ground and looked like bulbs, bright and flaky with white warts. The caps of others had lost color and spread into soiled platters seven inches wide. "Poisonous," I thought, "mushrooms that would add a fillip to the elderberry wine served by the murderous Brewster sisters in *Arsenic and Old Lace*."

Thought ripples, brushing across hours then folding back before drifting on or swirling and disappearing. On Thursday as I talked about *Walden*, I wondered if I was the only member of the English Department who doesn't wear underpants in the summer. Certainly I am the only person who teaches in carpet slippers, a reddish pair of "Tender Footsies" purchased by Vicki at Zeller's on Starrs Road in Yarmouth. I haven't filled a trophy case with prizes and fellowships. "You've written millions of words," Vicki said as she handed me the slippers. "If anybody has earned the right to teach in carpet slippers, you have."

My elsewheres are often poetic. On Monday when pretty brown-eyed Betty asked a question, I pondered the evanescence of beauty and thinking of Walter Savage Landor mumbled,

> Past ruin'd Ilion Helen lives,
> Alcestis rises from the shades;
> Verse calls them forth; 'tis verse that gives
> Immortal youth to mortal maids.

Rarely do I complete a poem. In life few things are completed. Behind one end lurks another end. For students the concept of finishing is a hypnotizing delusion, provoking them to impose morals and construct distorting summaries.

Much of the verse I recite focuses on loss and death. In contrast love poetry seems insignificant and has little to do with my actual life. For my part, although love poems appeal to students, I cannot read them without smothering a yawn. Fifty years ago my loves may have been like red, red roses. Newly sprung June has become late November, however, and powdery mildew, petal blight, and root rot, in fact a pest house of horticultural diseases, have sent my hankerings for Alba and Bourbon, Rambler and Tea, to the compost pile. Two weeks ago while a boy talked passionately about curbing irrigation in California so that the Colorado River would again reach the sea, I silently recited a stanza written by Christina Rossetti.

> When I am dead, my dearest,
> Sing no sad songs for me;
> Plant thou no roses at my head,
> Nor shady cypress tree:
> Be the green grass above me
> With showers and dew drops wet:
> And if thou wilt, remember,
> And if thou wilt, forget.

I don't remember the name of the boy who wanted to "free the Colorado," as he put it. No longer do I recall people's names, not something that causes me any discomfort other than a flicker of embarrassment. Moreover in order to write a person withdraws from other people, and seceding from cacophonous society, talks quietly to himself. In contrast to forgetting people's names, being unable to remember the names of flowers and trees lessens my world and upsets me. When words vanish, life browns into dieback. Of course, teaching forces me to mull age. The first day of term the vitality of students seemed boundless, and I thought of the initial stanza of May Swenson's "Question."

> Body my house
> my horse, my hound
> what will I do
> when you are fallen.

Silent ponderings do not make me melancholy. I have aged beyond susceptibility to gloom. Although the window frames bang and the walls of my house tremble in a high wind, I know what to do. I don't need to lay a new foundation or raise a trellis of girders to shore up my slack muscles and stabilize my thinning bones. At Canadian Tire this summer I read a sign advertising the miracle cures of WD-40. "2000 Uses," the advertisement declared, "Stops Squeaks, Loosens Rusted Parts, Drives Out Moisture" and "Frees Sticky Mechanisms." Although I rattle, not squeak, when I jog, WD-40 could probably restore my parts to working middle-age order. A few of my joints are rusted or at least their mechanisms stick. Mildew has settled into moist cracks in my feet, and some days I suffer from the pip. Unfortunately the advertisement did not prescribe dosages or provide instructions for taking the medicine, either orally or intravenously, I assume not in a suppository, the sign being in Canada. If the WD-40 failed to invigorate, I could buy a zinc anode at Waterview Marine Supplies and stop corrosion by attaching it to my hull, as a sign noted—hull being, I am sure, a euphemism for back and undersides. In any case decades spent luffing the Sea of Domesticity corrodes more than the bottomlands. The problem is that even a modest anode, one eight inches long, three wide, and one and a half thick, is too weighty for the ordinary tailbone. Never mind, a trip to Bulk Barn can furnish the medicine cabinet with other cure-alls. A handful of wasabi covered peanuts or a swig of Pomberry Blast, a blend of blueberry and pomegranate crystals, will likely cause the enervated to shout "Kamchatka" and leap to their feet. If the peanuts and crystals fail to produce a reaction, one can bolt a regimen of gummies. There are more kinds of gummies in Bulk Barn than there are varieties of antibiotics in a hospital, my favorites being juicy teeth gummies and juicy rattlesnake gummies. The former resembles false teeth of the maxillary kind, eight white teeth set in lingerie-pink gums, the latter seven yellow rattles attached to a tail more colorful than a barber's pole, blue, yellow, red, orange, and green.

Of course, students' minds are not always in the room with their bodies. At the beginning of every class, I attempt to clap mind and body together. Often I startle, in hopes of hooking thought, reeling it in from Never-Never Land. Last week I ordered people using laptop computers to sit in the first and second row of desks. "I do not tolerate looking at pornography," I said, "something, I hear, that is encouraged by many departments at this university." More often than not, however, my bait does not appeal to students. I have lost my faith in aliens, and reaction was mute on Friday when I said plaintively, "The United States is in terrible shape. Endless war has bankrupted the nation. Unemployment has wrecked millions of lives and caused the deaths of thousands of people. The country has become as tribal as the Balkans. Each region hates all the other regions. Never have we so needed the help of aliens. Why won't they come to our aid? Why have they forsaken us?" "Do you believe in aliens, Mr. Pickering?" little Michelle asked after I paused. I didn't answer. My mind was elsewhere. I was wondering if the lemon really is a Chinese symbol for death. If the fish represents Jesus and Christianity, then squeezing lemon on halibut is sacrilegious not culinary, a realization that should spur piscatorial aficionados to reform their dining habits. By not seasoning fish, they just might escape dessert, in Tartarus ice cream served a la mode, the eternal flavor molten lead.

Committed

America's leading exports are t-shirts and slogans. Last week the dean of a business school in Massachusetts returned from a trip to Mumbai. He reported that bumper stickers were extraordinarily popular in the Bandra Kurla, or financial district. The stickers resembled those often seen in the United States, the most popular emending "God Bless America" to "May the Gods Bless India" in order to appeal to the rupee-conscious Hindu population of Maharashtra. Two such stickers appeared on many cars, usually on the right and left sides of the rear bumper. On a gold Rolls Royce parked outside the offices of Citigroup, the dean counted four stickers, two on the front bumper and two on the back. Because sloganeering strains mind and back less than acting, boosterism thrives in the United States, especially in academic communities which endlessly congratulate themselves on their future accomplishments, clothes-pinning soggy weights of vapor to the tagline "Committed to Excellence." "Enough babbitry," my friend Josh exclaimed recently, in his hand holding a broadside celebrating the university's devotion to superlatives. "The Kingdom of Heaven is not at hand. Is Oxford really the Connecticut of Great Britain? A publication like this has nothing to do with reality," he said. "It reminds me of the bantam who believed the sun rose every morning just to listen to his crowing. Why doesn't someone acknowledge that the best college teachers are committed to mediocrity?"

For a fictional being Josh is persuasive although I frequently disagree with him. Excellence, though, often leads to smugness and undermines humbling self-knowledge. The more a person succeeds, the more success becomes him. His world constricts, and it is difficult for his imagination to bolt the paddock of convention. Eventually he loses himself and becomes one of those anybodies who is everybody. On the other hand the less seriously a person takes life and the more indifferent he is to fortune, the happier he will probably be. Since avoiding one's own company is impossible, a person should make himself his best companion. How pleasant it is to spend days in the congenial presence of the unambitious. Instead of struggling to climb Jacob's Ladder in hopes of tumbling into Abraham's bosom at some distant date, how much better to enjoy the present lolling atop the soft earth, sweet Nellie's poitrine a pillow. "The bee devotes its whole life to preparing for the next generation. But what is the next generation going to do?" A. A. Milne asked in *If I May*. "It is going to spend its whole life preparing for the third generation...and so on forever. An admirable community, the moralists tell us. Poor moralists!"

"To miss so much of the joy of life, to deny oneself the pleasure (to mention only one among many) of reclining lazily on one's back in a snapdragon, watching the little white clouds sail past upon a sea of blue; to miss these things for no other reason than that the next generation may also have an opportunity of missing them—is this admirable?" Milne continued. "What do the bees think they are doing? If they live a life of toil and self-sacrifice merely in order that the next generation may live a life of equal toil and self-sacrifice, what has been gained? Ask the next bee you meet what it thinks it is doing in this world, and the only answer it can give you is 'Keeping up the supply of bees.' Is that an admirable answer?"

Fortunately mediocrity often seeks people out and saves them from their ruinous selves, transforming busy-bee weeks into grasshopper moments. The first indication that the immune system has neutralized pathogens threatening their host with ambition is that a person's reading changes. One banishes Russian novels from the bedside table, replacing them with a stack of detective stories. "As thoughtful citizens we are hemmed in now by gigantic problems that appear as insoluble as they are menacing, so how pleasant it is to take an hour or two off to consider only the problem of the body that locked itself in its study and then used the telephone," J. B. Priestley wrote in *Delight*. "This is easy and sensible compared with the problem of remaining a sane citizen in the middle of the twentieth century. After the newspaper headlines, it is refreshing to enter this well-ordered microcosm, like finding one's way into a garden after wandering for days in a jungle."

Diminutive literary achievement attracts me. I never sigh wishing I had written *The Idiot* or *The Brothers Karamasov*. Instead I dream of fashioning the odd phrase, say, something comparable to Robert Macnish's description of the phlegmatic drunkard whose "ideas are as frozen as if concocted in the bowels of Lapland." Or better Gerald Gould's changing the first line of Robert Louis Stevenson's "Fifteen men on a dead man's chest" so that it read "Fifteen hairs on the cave man's chest." Would I had quipped that I gave "no credence to the statement there was honor among thieves. Crooks are as bad as the rest of us." I wish I were the anonymous person to whom Edmund Pearson attributed a limerick in *Books in Black and Red*. Authorship would have made me an eternal flame burning incandescently through the pages of *The Unabridged History of Connecticut Literature*.

> There was a young lady named Maud,
> And she was a terrible fraud;
> To eat at the table
> She never was able,
> But out in the pantry—Oh, Lawd!

Never do I imagine that my foxy view of macroeconomics will startle brokers into uncontrolled cackling. Instead I dream of chopping conversations off with puns, perhaps with a sentence such as "teetotalers come to their biers at the end" or maybe with a question, "Why is a man who looks at a giantess like a Roman emperor?" The answer is obvious: "because he sees her, the great." I don't mull the hoary question, "Who ate Newton's apple?" The truth is that no one ate it. In the second volume (1732) of the *Gentleman's Magazine* appeared a short article based on a letter Newton wrote his friend William Whiston, the Lucasian Professor of Mathematics at Cambridge. In the letter Newton said he threw the apple away. He explained that the apple was infested with sawflies, and when sliced open, exuded an odor "as unpleasant as that of a close stool." Occasionally a poetic fit seizes me, and I imagine writing a stanza or two, nothing sublime like the poetry described by Longinus, however. "For that is really great which bears a repeated examination," Longinus wrote, "and the memory of which is strong and hard to efface." The mind resembles a beaker. When too much is dumped into it, mind overflows causing debilitating anxiety. Any poetry I wrote would be mediocre and thus salubrious, leaking from thought during reading. Of course volumes of healthy, purgative verse already exist. Yesterday I ran across a particularly quick-acting quatrain.

> This is the house that Jesus built,
> And he built it without a hammer or nail,
> And in this house sinners lay down their sins,
> And drink the grace of the Lord by the pail.

Of course many readers prefer verse which treats the body rather than the spirit. Such readers hanker for poems into which they can drill quickly, and from which they can extract themselves painlessly—rhyming Novocain like the following stanza keeping them pleasantly sedated.

> A dentist, love, makes teeth of bone
> For those whom fate has left without,
> And finds provision for his own,
> By pulling other people's out.

In the nineteenth century memory jugs were popular. Victorians covered stoneware with an adhesive, often putty. Into the putty they stuck bric-a-brac, creating friezes of mementoes. The jugs I've seen are ugly, blackened as if their lasting depended upon lying forgotten, buried between insulation and floor boards in ratty attics, the knickknacks on their surfaces hardened into mats of dusty metallic fur. Once upon a time the jugs bristled quick, and their exteriors awakened recollection, bringing to mind intoxicating but ordinary memories, as the people who fashioned the jugs usually led modest lives: a thimble, a snippet of ribbon, a mourning ring, a lead soldier, the barrel of his rifle broken in half, the bowl of a souvenir teaspoon bought in Niagara Falls, and the head of a hen snapped off the lid of a milk glass salt dish. For my seventieth birthday, the children treated Vicki and me to three days at a bed and breakfast in Provincetown. Neither of us had ever been to Cape Cod, and from the long weekend we returned home carrying a jug tacky but alive with everyday memories, trinkets from mediocre hours happily spent. In my classes I urge students to read books for extra credit. I supply a list of volumes, none of which have much to do with the subject of the course. Most of the books are mediocre. Literarily they are third or fourth rate. However, all are "infectiously happy." For a moment or two after reading them a person feels content, and if the reader resembles me, says aloud to himself and to others who happen to be nearby, "Gee, life is swell." Among the books I suggest is Jean Webster's fairy tale, *Daddy-Long-Legs*. "It isn't the great big pleasures that count the most; it's making a great deal out of the little ones—I've discovered the true secret of happiness," Judy, the heroine, wrote in Daddy-Long-Legs, "and that is to live in the *now*. Not to be forever regretting the past, or anticipating the future; but to get the most that you can out of this very instant."

In Provincetown Vicki and I stayed in the carriage house behind the Fairbanks Inn, originally built in the 1770s for a sea captain. We roamed the city, meandering from east to west between Commercial and Bradford streets. Blocks of houses looked like platters of petite fours, flipped to one side then righted, some tumbling onto and sticking atop others, still others sliding wedged into nibbling spaces. The houses smacked of the traditional petite fours of New England—almond, cherry, orange, chocolate, and marzipan. Icings were varied and buttery. Doors and shutters were wafers of red, blue, gray, khaki, and green while fences were braids of meringue: spindle, lattice, scalloped Deerfield, Princeton, Newburyport Garden, and pickets, Sudbury, Yorktown, Chestnut Hill, and Nantucket among rails of others, most of these vanilla.

Vicki and I munched through hours eating bouillabaisse at the Lobster Pot, sampling Connie's sweet rolls, at Karoo Kafe drinking Tusker, a Kenyan beer, while eating samosas and falafel, kibbi and grape leaves. We invigorated ourselves with gelato at the Purple Feather Café and Treatery. Decades of sweet hankerings have made me an expert on "treateries." The Dairy Bar serves scrumptious ice cream in Storrs, while Ashley's dishes up the best in New Haven. In Storrs I always have a child's cone of chocolate brownie fudge. When I am out of town on a spree, I shred concern about cholesterol and have a regular, two-scoop cone, in New Haven sweet cream atop chocolate-

chocolate chip and in Provincetown almond crunch on dark chocolate.

We explored art galleries, viewing and coveting but not buying, a tree "surgeon" in Storrs having lopped off our play money. Provincetown raised our spirits, and Vicki and I drifted close, out of proper public distance, holding hands as we walked. Early October is off-season, and streets were not crowded. Our visit coincided with Mates Leather Weekend, however, and chaps, cowboy and motorcycle boots, vests, chains, and spiked collars were in fashion. Three species of couple wandered the town: men with men, women with women, and lastly men with women. All were my people, that is, middle-aged and older. The last night we ate dinner at Bayside Betsy's. In order to make eating easier the man next to me removed his leash and curled it up on the seat between us. He wore a pair of snug leather trousers. "I got them at the leather swap last night," he said. "I paid only $150 for them." A friend, he explained, had gained weight since last year, and when he returned for leather weekend this October, he couldn't fit into the trousers. Many people walked dogs. Corgis were the most popular breed. One old fellow in his eighties had donned leather overalls. His hips had corkscrewed loose from his spine, and he listed to the left. In his left hand he clutched a metal cane. In his right he held a leash, leading a brown Chihuahua. The dog was also old, and she limped, sinking to her right, not left. She, too, was dressed for the weekend. Circling her neck was a black leather collar, its studs polished and gleaming.

We rarely rested. We climbed Pilgrim Monument atop High Pole Hill, a hundred and sixteen steps and sixty ramps. The architecture was Italianate. "Nothing of dour Puritan about it," Vicki said. Plaques donated by societies composed of people descended from passengers on the *Mayflower* lined the tower. The societies were located in many states: Pennsylvania,

Michigan, New York, New Jersey, Colorado, Illinois, and California among others. "Theirs is not an ancestry I'd brag about," Vicki said. "Me neither," I said, adding that I might change my mind if the societies were located in more interesting places, Goa or Paraguay. More to our liking were the commemorative stones at "The First Landing Place" at Stevens Point. Carved into the faces of the stones were memorial inscriptions, "Life is a Song, So Sing Along," "One of the Kindest Souls, To Grace God's Earth," "Somewhere Over the Rainbow," and "No Matter What They Say, Truly in Love, Truly Gay." One evening we started to walk the breakwater to the lighthouse at Wood End. A storm in the Atlantic pushed the tide high, and after half a mile, we stopped as waves thumped over the rocks. For a time, we stood and stared out to sea. Close to shore salt marsh cord grass grew loose and rackety; farther out stretched meadows of salt marsh hay, channels weaving between them, turning the little islands into pieces of a green jigsaw puzzle. In the distance the sky was luminous. Pale yellow lay like straw low on the horizon. Above the yellow curved a band of silver, this topped by a soothing blue expanse.

One morning we rented bicycles from P'town Bikes on Bradford Street. We cycled along Moors Road to Herring Cove Beach then followed bike trails twisting for seven miles through the sandy outwash plains of Cape Cod National Seashore Park. Some flowers lingered into autumn, a few shafts of seaside goldenrod and thin clusters of asters. Pitch pines grew bristly beside the trails, among them scrub oaks. Great black-backed gulls strutted the shoreline at Race Point Beach while terns darted across and under the wind. Vicki and I ate lunch at a picnic table near the Province Lands Visitor Center, eating a hard-boiled egg and a Macoun apple apiece and sharing a bologna sandwich. Above and around us blue jays scrabbled through the tops of the pines. Afterward we cycled through the

Beech Forest and back to Provincetown. "A great morning, what a good birthday present," Vicki said after we returned the bicycles to the shop.

Academic puffery celebrates the "problem solver," rarely noting that solutions invariably create new problems. Rather than straining to direct life's parade, the devotee of mediocrity simply appreciates the passing pageantry. As sunshine is a multitude of small beams, so the small and the ordinary warm days. "I am one of those people," my student Emily wrote, "who dresses her dog in little hot pink outfits speckled with rhinestones. My dog Booboo has a cowgirl hat with Velcro straps that go under her muzzle, a Christmas sweater with a jingle bell sewed onto the neck line, and her own wall calendar. In July she appears sitting in front of a giant American flag with a smaller flag clenched between her teeth." "I never buy clothes," Wilson stated. "Early Sunday morning I walk the party thoroughfares on campus and scavenge shirts, shorts, and trousers discarded during the night. Sometimes I wonder what provokes people to abandon their clothes in the winter, but I don't really care. I don't have any spare money, and I need clothes. Moreover scavenging is a good way to remain well-dressed. Fraternity boys are fashion-conscious, and I find my best outfits outside fraternity houses. I have received many compliments on my appearance."

"When I was in primary school," Masie said, "I played the violin in my backyard at night. I arranged lawn chairs in a half circle and put my stuffed animals, Barbie dolls, and my brother's Ninja Turtle action figures in the seats. The milky light of the stars illuminated my practice book, and I saw the scales better than I did in the house. I was not afraid of the dark because I was not alone. I knew that all around the world girls were playing music in the moonlight." The mediocre life is not small; sweetness and light endlessly brighten its hours. "Most people don't live; they just race," Judy wrote in *Daddy-Long-Legs*. In the heat of trying "to reach some goal far away on the horizon," they "lose all sight of the beautiful, tranquil country they are passing through; and the first thing they know, they are old and worn out, and it doesn't make any difference whether they have reached the goal or not."

"Are you really committed to mediocrity?" a student in my essay class asked last month. "Yes," I said. "Great," she said, "That means I don't have to worry about sounding profound. I can tell the truth and write about what interests me." The girl was a flanker on the women's rugby team. Three days later she handed in her essay. "I have a competitive streak that has been running since birth," she began. "While my older sister was born through a C-section, I scored on my first try, right down the birth canal. I still hold the record among my siblings as the only natural delivery and also the record for the highest birth weight. To this day a walk to the car with my brother always evolves into a race. Over the summer I worked at a home for men with developmental disabilities. Virtual bowling was a favorite pastime. I was forced to limit my participation because I got into too many arguments with a resident over which one of us was the rightful victor in the games we played." "What did you think?" the girl asked me the next week. "A try and a conversion," I said.

Morning Sickness

For decades reading the newspaper at breakfast nauseated me. A glance at the contents and my mood turned dun while bile began to percolate, its grounds rough and almost tinny, as if my feelings were being shoveled into a burr mill. That has changed. A month ago I canceled my subscription to the morning paper. Now at breakfast I sip a cordial of poetry. The poems are not nepenthes, intoxicating and distancing me from life. Instead the verse awakens and broadens sensibilities. Amid the granola, bananas, soy milk, and Russian tea, I pause and, if I don't smile, I nod, in the pleasure of words finding harmony. The world is always muddled, but living doesn't have to be as confused as the front page of a newspaper, a surreal blend of pathos and absurdity, of gossip and propaganda, of commerce, and of packaged heartache oozing artificial sweetener.

Now at breakfast Lydian airs freshen my spirit, and Childe Roland's approaching the dark tower is endlessly suggestive. Sometimes between spoons of All Bran I hum native wood notes wild and sport with Amaryllis in the shade. Spring is months away, but when it arrives, weeds will spin in wheels and "shoot long and lovely and lush." Besides, beauty is wondrously present and ever-dappled no matter the season when I read lines like Meredith's:

> Lovely are the curves of the white owl sweeping
> Wavy on the dusk lit by one large star.
> Lone on the fir-branch, his rattle-note unvaried,
> Brooding o'er the gloom, spins the brown evejar.

As black type demanding attention and trumpeting importance vanishes from the morning, so perspective changes. "Greatness of soul," Montaigne wrote, "is not so much pressing upward and forward as knowing how to set oneself in order and circumscribe oneself. It regards as great whatever is adequate and shows its elevation by liking moderate things better than eminent ones." The more modest the mansion the soul builds, to emend Oliver Wendell Holmes, the more satisfactory the life.

The view from a modest house is rational and comparatively happy. The owner realizes that no alterative can purge nationalism from the world, and that war and its cruel devices will always be "too much with us." "We often learn, when it is too late," L. P. Jacks wrote resignedly in 1917, "that the existence of an instrument for performing an action is the cause of that action being performed." Yet, when one imagines *The Mikado*'s three little maids skipping away from school "filled to the brim with girlish glee" and eavesdrops on *Patience* and hears Bunthorne singing about "a most particularly pure young man," pessimism and paralyzing spleen slip from mind, neither of them to "be missed." "I do not see what is wrong with being hostile and contemptuous toward one's fellow creatures," Gerald Gould declared in *All About Women*. "It is the attitude I am always trying to cultivate for myself." Gould's remark is an amalgam of the playful and the serious. Still, Gould was a journalist and every day observed the sad and the foolish. For my part since I quit reading the newspaper, I have thought better of my fellows. Although poetry has not made me an optimist, blighted expectation will not cause me to throw myself into a depression exclaiming, "Oh, willow, titwillow, titwillow."

In "Walking" Thoreau said there was a need for a "Society for the Diffusion of Useful Ignorance." Knowledge is conventional and often so distracting that it obscures vision and prevents people from thinking and knowing. I didn't vote in last week's town elections, the only election in which I haven't voted since settling in Storrs thirty-five years ago. I missed both the election and turning the clocks back, switching them out of Daylight Savings Time. I had not kept up because I no longer read the newspaper. I neglected nothing significant. In Ecclesiastes, the preacher mentions a time to be born and a time to die. I managed the first well, causing Mother little pain, and I'm not worried about the second. Although he ranges broadly, alluding to a time to cast away stones and a time to sew, the preacher ignores the time to reset clocks or for that matter getting to class on time. No matter the time zone, Eastern, Central, or Daylight, I am always in the classroom thirty minutes before lessons are scheduled to start. Insofar as voting is concerned, breaking the harness of political palaver is the most telling benefit of banishing the news from the kitchen table. Tonguing with me, tonguing with thee, and tonguing with everybody, as the old saying puts it, grinds intelligence out of thought and beauty out of words. In his youth, C. E. Montague recounted, he fell in love with words, "the mellow fullness or granular hardness of their several sounds, the balance, the undulation or trailing fall of their syllables, or the core of sun like splendor in the broad, warm central vowel of such a word as 'auroral.'" Political speech denatures language, and is, my friend Josh thinks, the cause of America's having "the largest illiterate reading public in the world."

In "Old England," A. C. Benson conceded that living in the past could be a mistake. "But the old life had a beauty and stillness of its own," he wrote, "when there was less motion and stir, less sound and foam; there was less arranging how to live, and more acceptance of life." In part I rid myself of the paper in hopes of deadening the clatter of insistent moments. I wanted to live in a quieter, perhaps older, by-gone place in which the foam of small event did not rise and smother. I imagined looking out the window and not seeing people scurrying like formicidae. I hoped to see lasting loveliness, not the evanescent motion of ambition. At the end of October a snow storm swept across Connecticut, blasting trees and felling power lines. Restoring electricity took ten days. Pouting dominated newspapers, and radio waves lengthened into shrill whines. Suckled on the instant gratification of the Internet, people demanded that power companies complete their repairs three days before yesterday. Few people accepted that sudden disruptive events were a part of life. Instead of enduring misfortune gracefully, maybe by reading poetry during the daylight, they unleashed arrows of outraged blame, making themselves contemptuous and making me long for a poetic diverter, say, the soothing sound of Tennyson's Lotus Land.

> There is sweet music here that softer falls
> Than petals from blown roses on the grass,
> Or night-dews on still waters between walls
> Of shadowy granite, in a gleaming pass;
> Music that gentlier on the spirit lies,
> Than tired eyelids upon tired eyes;
> Music that brings sweet sleep down from the blissful skies.
> Here are cool mosses deep,
> And through the moss the ivies creep,
> And in the stream the long-leaved flowers weep,
> And from the craggy ledge the poppy hangs in sleep.

In March when mud and windbags arrive in splenetic force, I will recite Housman and be content.

> Loveliest of trees, the cherry now
> Is hung with bloom along the bough,
> And stands about the woodland ride
> Wearing white for Eastertide.

In an old tale a road split in a dark wood. One fork turned left, the other right. A sign stood beside each fork. On both signs an arrow pointed into the dark; under each arrow were the words, "This Way to Hell." One day a party of pilgrims reached the fork. They stopped and conferred, after which one half the pilgrims took the left road, the other the right. A single traveler remained at the fork after his compatriots departed. He stood for a time then he stepped off the road and plunged into the woods, pushing his way through briars and brambles. "To be a perfectly honest writer," Edwin Muir wrote in *Latitudes*, "one thing is essential, one must not have a system." Newspapers steer readers. Their columns don't lead to Hell, but rarely do the thoughts of readers soar above the "Aonian Mount." Amid bushes far from editorial and sports pages, advertisements for resorts, recipes, and weeks in review, one escapes partisan narrowness and the confines of systematic living. Louise Glück began her poem "Messengers," writing, "You have only to wait, they will find you. / The geese flying low over the marsh, / glittering in black water. / They find you."

The wait is rarely long. Once morning sickness vanishes, a person's hours seem winged. Things that would have probably been lost amid the roll of papers I now notice and find satisfyingly suggestive. Odd words and phrases stick to mind, marsh rabbit, for example, the country name for muskrat. Every day David, my running companion, uses a word, the meaning of which I don't know. In the past the hard pace of running erased definitions. Now the words not only find me, but they stay with me, yesterday's word being *callipygian* or having shapely, oh, heck, scrumptious buttocks. Recently my old friend Houston wrote me. Houston is ninety-three. His wife died more than twenty years ago. "Several months ago," Houston wrote, "I had a strange experience. I was in bed and dreaming that my dear wife and I were talking happily when I heard the telephone ring.

In the dream I got up and answered the phone. It was a wrong number. When I returned to bed, my wife had disappeared. I missed her, and the dream continued for more than a few minutes. Then the real phone rang. I awoke and answered it. It was a wrong number." Real life appears when a person crumples the "lifestyle" pages. "My father," an older student recounted, "was a postman with arthritic knees and tired feet. His work boots were like fossils. When he came home late at night, the dim lights in the house made the circles under his eyes look like cereal bowls full of Coca Cola."

I am gregarious, but Vicki is shy. We don't entertain other people, and some folks think us reclusive. Occasionally somebody says I am stand-offish, a criticism that bothers me. "You should ignore such remarks," my old schoolmate Eddie wrote me. "Poetry is enough." In his letter Eddie included an excerpt from Max Beerbohm's *And Even Now*. "Lions do not ask one another to their lairs, nor do birds keep open nest. Certain wolves and tigers, it is true, have been so seduced by man from their natural state that they will deign to accept man's hospitality. But when you give a bone to your dog, does he run out and invite another dog to share it with him?—and does your cat insist on having a circle of other cats around her saucer of milk?"

Although the hounds of winter are on autumn's traces, the year in Connecticut is between seasons. One afternoon Indian summer is balmy on the breeze. During the night Jack Frost saunters across the hills, and the next morning window panes are silvery as wood smoke. Academic terms emphasize the seasonal. The first semester begins in September as summer heat slides below the hills and ends the week before Christmas. The second starts in frozen January only to stop just as mud season dries into flowers. Students are preternaturally aware of change, relentlessly observing themselves and the school year. "In New

England," Andy wrote in his last paper, "coffee shops cater to the seasons, serving green-tinted drinks in the spring and in the summer icy brews flavored with coconut. All things pumpkin appear in the fall, and snow flurries of peppermint dust the winter. Despite the obvious silliness, consumers connect the passing of time with drinks as much as with physical changes in their surroundings. Falling leaves means that the pumpkin spice latte will be back at Starbucks like the blowing of peonies signals the transition between spring and summer." The end of the fall semester always elicits reflections on holidays, the comments more poignant than "human interest" inserts in Sunday papers. "I liked Christmas more than Thanksgiving, but not by much," Emily wrote, reminiscing. "I was never as excited as the other kids in school. In first and second grade we spent a week making paper snowflakes and reindeer candy canes. All I ever did was cut triangles out of paper, and my snowflakes were always ugly. I resented my classmates' intricate designs and perfectly placed googly eyes."

Teachers give sundry reasons for retiring. "Papers, those damn papers," Richard said. "I couldn't grade another paper." Some teachers retire because they have broken physically while others who are vigorous explain that they want to retire before they begin to slip mentally. "I'm quitting while I am still at the top of my game," Mickey told me in the gymnasium. Still others echo Thoreau on leaving his cabin at Walden and declare they have other lives to live. These people usually plan to travel, something a handful accomplish. In a few folks the curmudgeon sets in early, and they cease to believe that teaching accomplishes anything. They claim that no abuse can ever be eradicated and that the paths they bushwhacked through social swamps will inevitably be overgrown and return to weed and injustice, ignorance and thorn. Last spring Kate retired with a biting flourish. She hung her keys to the arts building on a hook in the secretary's office then quoted Ivor Brown's definition of education as "casting sham pearls before real swine." Perhaps, however, most teachers retire because classes, especially the liveliest and brightest classes, eventually make a person melancholic. Students' pasts are immediate, and they write easily about growing up. My own children have grown distant. Whenever I think about their childhoods, those years when ice cream cones made their hearts leap in joy, I become sad, and life seems diminished. Better it is for my calm of mind for honeyed memory to lie buried. I don't want to resemble Tennyson's Rizpah and hear the past calling "come out to me." Students' essays dig through the crusts of time like dredges and lift buried emotions into the present, bringing smiles to the lips but aching to the breast. "One year when I was little," Amy wrote in her last essay, "I made a tiny box as a present for my parents. I wrapped it in shiny red paper and hung it on the Christmas tree. In the box I put a folded piece of paper on which I wrote, 'Deer Mommy and Daddy, Hav a Mary Crismis, Love Amy.'" After I read Amy's essay, I couldn't breathe. I remembered a Christmas when Edward constructed six tiny books for me and hung them on our tree. On the front of each book he drew a dog. "Gone, gone," I mumbled as I held Amy's paper, "all gone, damn it to hell."

"You have only to let it happen," Louise Glück wrote. I have followed her instructions, and untold things have found me. Moreover not reading a newspaper hasn't caused me to miss any exciting happenings. Last Saturday Vicki and I attended the "Grand Opening" of the Petco store across route 195 opposite East Brook Mall in the building once occupied by a Salvation Army outlet. Shoppers brought dogs to the opening, and I counted a pack of fourteen standing near the checkout counter. A woman led a pet guinea pig about on a blue leash. The guinea pig wore a red plaid harness, and after setting him under a stocking cap, the sort worn by one of Santa's helpers, a photographer took a picture of him. Petco was a pet fancier's supermarket, selling among shelves of other things, clothes, foods, a pharmacy of diet supplements, "boredom busters," "sweet rewards," "shoe savers," and "plush toys," these last "your best friend's other best friend." PetSafe's bark control collars were on sale. The Deluxe model for a big dog cost $119.99, while the same model for a small dog went for $98.99. One aisle was a furniture store of beds: pillow, cuddler, round nesting, and orthopedic. Wag-a-Tude's "New Fall Apparel" was in stock. Hats and scarves started at $6.99 and hoodies at $14.99. Jackets cost $19.99. A jacket for girlie girl dogs was pink with a fur collar and came in multiple sizes, the "XX Small," for example, recommended for teacup poodles, Chihuahuas, and Yorkshire terriers. Vicki and I did not purchase anything, but we didn't leave empty-handed. We carried out a box of food samples, from Merrick, a bag of Grammy's Pot Pie, "a Home Cooked Memory Made with Real Chicken, Hearty Whole Grains, and Merrick Elements," and a can of Thanksgiving Day Dinner, "A Home Style Dog Entrée," containing turkey, sweet potatoes, green beans, carrots, and Granny Smith apples. "That was good fun," Vicki said as we walked back to the car. "A super morning," I answered, "better than any celebration described in a Living section." "You mean Dying section," Vicki replied.

Saturday afternoon I raked the yard, a seasonal chore I dread, the high point always an encephalitic chat with a neighbor out for a stroll. "Raking leaves, are you?" the neighbor invariably begins. "Yep," I answer, "but I sure hate doing it." "I know what you mean," the neighbor responds, "but you have to do it, don't you?" "You're right. I have to do it," I say, "better now than later." "Boy, that's the truth. You hit the nail smack on the head," the neighbor answers, adding, "Well, I best be off and leave you to it. You'll want to finish before Christmas." "You can say that again," I reply, "take care." "You, too, have a good one," the neighbor says, turning away. This year the expected conversation and piles of leaves were lighter than usual. The poetry I sipped at the breakfast table alleviated raking lethargy along with morning sickness. In "Snow" Charles Wright wrote, "If we, as we are, are dust, and dust, as it will, rises, / Then we will rise, and recongregate / In the wind, in the cloud, and be their issue." Corpses should be wrapped in cotton shrouds and buried near the surface of the ground, I thought as I raked. If that were done, their dust would rise easily up through roots and leaves. Lifted into clouds by wind, Mother and Father would always be close, falling into my life as spring rain or riding snowflakes in the winter helping to smother gloom and turning the world white. Perhaps they would be part of rainbows, maybe the yellow that always makes me hopeful. As the day passed and I raked through dusk, ache spiraled into my joints and muscles. I felt good, however. Leaves clung tightly to the sugar maple saplings and the understory of beeches at the edge of the yard, and I knew several more rakings lay ahead. The thought did not undermine my good spirits. The maples and beeches were stunningly orange and yellow. "I wonder if the soul is that lovely," I mused. As I stared bedazzled by the leaves, I thought of Mary Oliver's "Some Questions You Might Ask," one of my breakfast poems. In the poem Oliver pondered the soul, speculating about its appearance and about who and what possessed a soul. "What about the blue iris?" she asked, ending the poem. "What about all the little stones, sitting alone in the moonlight? / What about roses, and lemons, and their shining leaves? / What about the grass?" "They and these trees all have souls," I said to myself. "Their beauty brightens our long livings."

Tourist at Home

"At home we tolerate—sometimes even love—our fellow creatures. We can see large masses of them in church and theater, we can be jostled by them in streets, and be kept waiting by them in shops, and be inconvenienced by them at almost every turn, without rancorous annoyance or ill will," Agnes Repplier declared in *Compromises*. "But abroad it is our habit to regard all other travelers in the light of personal and unpardonable grievances. They are intruders into our chosen realms of pleasure, they jar upon our sensibilities, they lessen our meager share of comforts, they are everywhere in our way, they are always an unnecessary feature in the landscape." *Compromises* was published in 1904 when Repplier was 49 years old. If the book had appeared twenty years later when Repplier had reached the age I am now, she would not have treated folks at home so charitably. She would have aged into being an alien out of place and out of harmony with her surroundings.

On Friday I had my hearing tested. Although I won't hear the high fizzing of warblers again, my hearing is excellent, and I have no trouble understanding standard English. Unlike my hearing, English, however, has deteriorated into a bastardly mumble, sounding like a blend created by a disk jockey coked to the gills and wheeling a stove top of turn tables back and forth boiling syllables. If "a man's speech is the measure of his culture," I have little in common with the people that jostle me every day. Last week while riding my bicycle across the campus, I heard a boy address a girl saying, "I'm like, 'What the fuck's going on, dude?'" Once I enjoyed going to cafés with Vicki. Only rarely do we enjoy them now. Cafés have become anti-social hangouts. Students monopolize the tables, hunkered for hours over computers and cell phones, their "pretty toys," in Thoreau's words, "improved means to an unimproved end." They scowl and don't smile, and almost never do they speak or order more than a single cup of coffee. Fashion also jars my sensibilities. Youth dons shirts across the fronts of which are stamped the names of bands that I have not heard of and whose music I will never listen to unless I am condemned to spend eternity in Limbo, more aptly named "The Paradise of Fools." Even worse than adolescent attire is the carbuncular regalia of intimidation and superstition worn by adults—uniforms of repressive faiths and pinched, intolerant beliefs. "Conscience, not the devil, is the ape of God," Josh said recently, "its corruptions are more pervasive and more dangerous than those of the understanding."

Additionally, few contemporary amusements appeal to me. I cannot recognize celebrities, and I am not a fan of war, buncombe or sports. "The horrors of modern 'pleasure' arise from the fact that every kind of organized distraction tends to become more and more imbecile," Aldous Huxley wrote in *On the Margin*. "There was a time when people indulged themselves with distractions requiring the expense of a certain intellectual effort." No man can hoist himself above the low main, however, and three weeks ago I saw a soccer game. I won't attend a second contest. The afternoon was endless. By the conclusion of the game, my backside was numb. Moreover the people surrounding me were as lively as coal scuttles, the high-point of chit-chat being when a man on my left turned to me after a corner kick and said, "That was well-played, almost a goal." "Pretty close to one," I said. "You watch. We'll score before long," he replied. The man was a seer. Thirty-two minutes later, Connecticut scored, winning the game 1 to 0. "Didn't I tell you?" the man said after the goal. "You sure did," I said. "The educated American can get a living more easily than he can learn to live. The moral lessons are harder than the intellectual, and faith and enthusiasm, sympathy and imagination, are moral qualities," Bliss Perry said in *The American Spirit*. Aside from the risk of galloping bedsores brought on by sitting endlessly, being a fan makes no tough demands, enthusiasm not rising from within but orchestrated from without by loud speakers and television monitors.

If it were not for the rhythms of the seasons, I'd believe I lived in a foreign country. Flocks of robins are familiar sights now scrabbling across the ground. Squirrels blow in wind shears across the yard, their tails feather dusters. Deer amble casually across the street in front of the house, and after Thanksgiving Vicki put the turkey carcass atop the stone pile in the woods. For a day a hem of crows stitched through the trees. The next day the carcass disappeared, carried off by a coyote or perhaps a fisher. Mice have migrated inside, and, although I dislike doing so, I have set traps in the basement and baited them with peanut butter. During the day chipmunks carry hickory nuts through the crack in the foundation under the study then roll them about, the piles shifting and breaking in short snaps.

In 1935 Desmond MacCarthy opined that the person "who takes social distinctions very seriously may be a fool for doing so, but I cannot get up much indignation against that particular form of foolishness, especially when it has its roots in natural aesthetic preferences and sensibilities." Alas, I cannot escape social foolishness. To me habitués of café and bleacher seem no better than chicken dentists, making me long for the company of folks raised amid the high purple. Moreover as the ancient saying states, while some people are born young, many others are born old—these last appealing to me even though a few, as doctors put it in describing dementia, "have begun to run from their minds."

Age, Emerson wrote, "requires fit surroundings. Age is comely in coaches, in churches, in chairs of state and ceremony, in council-chambers, in courts of justice and historical societies.

Age is becoming in the country." Emerson believed Age should avoid the turmoil of street and town. For my part I think Age especially attractive on cruise boats. Only when I leave home and travel to fit surroundings, to differ with Repplier, can I tolerate or admire my fellow creatures. They enrich my chosen realms. Aged tourists are comfortable with words. "What did the person eat who dined on a lean wife and the ruin of man for a side dish," a jovial man asked me, answering his question when I looked puzzled, "A spare rib and apple sauce." A man who had read my books and who was wearing a pumpkin colored vest said that an evangelist set out on horseback from Nashville in hopes of saving the souls of folks living high in the hills above Carthage. One evening after a muddy day's riding, the man came upon a weary farmhouse. An old woman sat on the front porch rocking and drinking dandelion coffee. "Praise the Lord," the preacher said then got off his horse and addressed woman asking, "Sister, do you have religion?" "Well," the woman said, putting down the coffee, "I have slight touches of it occasionally, but it don't pain me much, and when it does, I takes a little tonic, one of these here fortified medicines made down to Difficult Creek. The rest of the time—Hallelujah—I'm strong temperance."

    Tourists my age who live in glass houses pull down the shades. *Likes* and *dudes* don't sweep revealingly through their speech in a dismal tide. Even their raw criticisms are cooked and stylish. "The son of a bitch is so lazy," a man on a cruise said describing a politician, "that he has to lean against a fence to bark." Conversation flows during meals and is not inhibited by the maxims that narrow the speech of the untutored. In the company of their contemporaries, aged talkers ignore cautionary couplets like, "Speak never of sickness, nor the death of a friend, / Not nauseous nostrums, till dinner shall end." Far from home, aged tourists are no longer aliens. Comfortable in themselves and with others, they become less censorious and simply enjoy the passing scene. "We read and travel," Huxley wrote, "not that we may broaden and enrich our minds, but that we may pleasantly forget they exist. We love reading and travelling because they are the most delightful of all the many substitutes for thought."

I have become an old bachelor, and Vicki has become both my maid and nurse, sweeping and scolding. I am fussy and intolerant of the culturally fetal and feral but withal dopily sentimental. In *Hope Farm Notes*, Herbert Collingwood told a swell weepy tale about a deaf farmer. Ever since the farmer and his wife lost their only baby, their lives had been grim. Then one day when the farmer was in town he saw a small, thin girl wearing tattered shoes, "a little black-haired thing with great brown eyes which carried the look of some hunted animal." The little girl noticed the farmer observing her and spontaneously reached out to grasp his hand. Immediately the girl's mother smacked her daughter's hand aside. The woman was sharp-faced and cruel, and her husband had abandoned her. The woman thought her daughter a brat and ached to be rid of her. The farmer consulted Lawyer Brown, and before the day ended the farmer adopted the girl. The farmer's wife initially opposed the adoption, but she softened as her husband grew gentle and loving. For a time, life was sunny, but then the little girl came down with a fatal fever. As she lay dying, she whispered something in the farmer's ear. Because he was deaf, however, he could not hear what she said. With her last strength, the girl wrote a sentence on a piece of paper and gave it to the farmer. The farmer put the paper in his pocket. Often in the weeks that followed, he produced the paper and read the sentence. No matter how laborious the day had been, the girl's words brought a "happy beautiful smile" to the man's face. His wife marveled at how reading the paper brightened her husband's mood, and one day she took the paper from his pocket and read what the little girl wrote: "I'll tell God how good you are."

Like other ancient bachelors who still have most of their marbles, I have outgrown superstitions. I don't tip my cap to history. I refuse to carry owls to Athens. I know the road to Parnassus cannot be measured in miles, and I no longer genuflect to numbers. No one can convince me that violets grow as tall as nettles. Neither black cats nor two-headed opossums intimidate me. Still, delusions entertain me, and I'd like to meet the witch who turns preachers into wind chimes. Rarely, though, do I stumble across the inexplicable, and if I do, I behave sensibly. I am not preternaturally brave, and if on some midnight amble I meet the dog that casts a white shadow, I'll yelp and scamper away. In the daylight, I am bolder. I growl and slam my door in the face of busybodies who visit at election time and insist on telling me voting is important. Vicki will feed me broccoli on my deathbed, but when I chew, I state the truth: broccoli has the texture of fuzzy grass. I think success results from a failure of the will to be free, and I admire people who have mastered floating on their backs in the Sea of Folly. I avoid academics who don't wish to be understood. On the other hand liars are often good-natured and benevolent, and I enjoy their company. I believe ignorance is the mother of devotion; yet, I also think principles are more dangerous for smart people than for fools. I don't care who plucks the last rose of summer, and I agree with the old saw, "It's a great life if you don't weaken."

But, of course, everybody and everything weakens, and things that don't weaken change in unappealing ways. The study of English is devolving into applied English, an oily matter of punctuated carburetors and declarative crankshafts that purport to tune up sputtering folks so they won't stray from lined convention. "I love a broad margin to my life," Thoreau recounted in *Walden*. "Sometimes, in a summer morning," he recounted, "I sat in my sunny doorway from sunrise till noon, rapt in a reverie, amidst the pines and hickories and sumacs, in undisturbed solitude and stillness, while the birds sang around or flitted noiseless through the house, until by the sun falling in at my west window, or the noise of some traveler's wagon on the distant highway, I was reminded of the lapse of time. I grew in those seasons like corn in the night." Once, studying English provided an occasion for reading and growing naturally, sometimes like corn, other times like pokeweed. Teachers of English knew that knowledge could not be quantified and resisted defining "a good education." Nowadays I feel like a stranger in a department in which I have taught for thirty-five years. The best way, for example, to appreciate Dante Gabriel Rossetti's "The Blessed Damozel" is by reading in a reverie, letting words shimmer, mysterious beyond parsing. The poem begins:

> The blessed damozel leaned out
> From the gold bar of heaven:
> Her eyes were deeper than the depth
> Of waters stilled at even;
> She had three lilies in her hand,
> And the stars in her hair were seven.

"Devotees of grammatical studies," Bronson Alcott wrote, "have not been distinguished for any remarkable felicities of expression." Alcott judged too harshly. For many years anthologies included a witty poem by the grammarian Ibn Malik, "The Pullet's First Prayer" which famously begins, "Now I lay me." The surest sign of old bachelordom is grumpiness. Actually I am not so much exasperated by the mechanical doings of grammarians as I am frustrated with writing itself. Not serpents but sentences wrapped themselves around Laocoön, poisoning him. According to Alvin Sanders in *In Winter Quarters*, Robert Burns "was not fit to live" around when writing. "At such times he was nervous, preoccupied, irritable, and absolutely impossible, from the standpoint of conventional society." For thirty-five years I have written steadily. Some days I get up before dawn to write. I cycle home between classes and write. I carry a reporter's notebook with me wherever I go and jot down observations. Writing keeps me bilious and impatient. At dinner I am preoccupied and am a poor table companion. I am tired of pens and pencils and want to escape the coils of this venomous diabolical possession. Maybe if Vicki and I leave Storrs for a while, I'll stop scribbling and become one of Huxley's dozy travelers. In shaping experience for the pages, writers miss much of life. "We begin to moralize and look wise, and Beauty, who is something of a coquette, and of an exacting turn of mind and likes attention," Alexander Smith wrote, "gets disgusted with our wisdom or our stupidity and goes off in a huff." On the other hand, slowing down might not be good for me. As the tread bare pun puts it, "a wheel runs best when it is tired."

Although I am a dyspeptic old bachelor, I have not jettisoned all my appetites. Last month my innards yowled when I read recipes for Smothered Muskrat, Horseshoe Crab with Tomato Tartar Sauce, and Doves Stuffed with Oysters. First dip the oysters in melted butter then roll them in bread crumbs before placing three in each bird, this last recipe advised. After dredging the doves in flour, smothering them with butter, and seasoning them with salt and pepper, place them, the instructions continued, in a roasting pan and "lard the breasts with thin slices of salt pork." Bake until tender and serve on a "bed of fine bread crumbs, crisped and browned in butter or over wild rice." Yummy! On the wings of a golden brown dove, the imagination soars, even that of a tourist at home, and I dream of wandering over the hills, say, to the eighteenth-century

India depicted in Thomas Daniell's paintings, "The Mountains of Ellora," or, for example, "Hindoo Temples at Bindrabund," their roofs rising in shady cones—or perhaps to John Glover's nineteenth-century Tasmania with the black trunks of his trees dancing like Mimi spirits. I am in better condition than Glover when he arrived in Tasmania. He was 64 years old, grossly overweight and had club feet. Alas, ease makes sluggards of us all, and I will never travel to India or Tasmania. Still, I must leave home and forswear scribbling; words are magnets which attract other words and dens of sentences.

Last week a stranger sent me a poem she found in an old periodical, asking me what I thought of it.

> Captain Corn in the garden
> Straight and strong and tall,
> No matter how high his neighbors grow,
> He overtops them all.
> He really cuts a dash;
> But when he marries Lima Bean,
> He'll lose his rank—I think it's mean—
> And be plain Succo Tash.

"You are a renowned literary agronomist," the woman wrote, "an expert in harvesting cornpone from poetic furrows." My correspondent's tone was winning, and I began an answer mentioning grits and hominy, Early Sunglow, Avalanche, and Country Gentleman. But then as phrases knotted and hissed, I stopped writing. "I must go down to the seas again," I said to myself. "All I want is a cruise boat and merry yarns from laughing fellow-rovers." I laid my pencil on the table and picked up the telephone. Ten minutes later I booked a Christmas cruise. Vicki and I will spend three vagrant weeks in the Caribbean—tourists at home away from home. Vicki says she intends to get tan as a cowbird and fat on all-you-can-eat pastries.

Afterword

My muse is dead. She didn't die a natural death. I strangled her and chopped her into bits then fed her to the dogs. For a while they scampered about glassy-eyed and barked in iambic pentameter. They dug perfectly round holes in the yard and in the morning folded the blankets in their beds. That behavior has passed, however. They have returned to being ordinary dogs, scratching, begging for snacks, cleaning their parts, and scooting their bottoms across the rugs in the living room. My muse was cruel and demanding. For decades, she tortured me. She refused to let me sleep. She jabbed pencils into me and woke me at 2:30 in the morning forcing me to go downstairs and write in the dark. She made me rush home between classes and scribble. She grabbed me by the scruff of the neck and jerked me away from the dinner table before Vicki served dessert. She made me swill coffee and sit locked at my desk until my legs cramped. She lied and toyed with me. She promised that my books would be popular. I told her that sales did not matter. All I hoped was that my writing would brighten a few people's lives. I didn't covet fame or fortune. I wanted in some way I couldn't articulate to be a force for goodness and decency. That was a silly delusion. Reviewers ignored my books. People I'd taught with since the beginning of time were astonished when they discovered that I had written more than a handful of pages. "Well," I thought, "to hell with paragraphs and pages, proper prose and sweetness 'lite.' Now that my muse has become dog shit, I am through with writing."

And I suppose that's it. You have just read my last book, and I feel pretty good. In fact before bedtime I'll hum "Kitty of Coleraine." Afterward I will sleep soundly. I'll dream of buttermilk watering the backyard. Not once will writing raise its nightmarish head. I will wake refreshed and ready to go. But what, I wonder, will I be ready for? I don't have hobbies. I am not sure what a ratchet is, and Vicki has forbidden all talk of a chain saw. I can't raise the hood of a car or patch a bicycle tire. I don't have enough money to disappear in the jungle on a long adventure. I don't watch television, and big-time athletics make me break out in hives and thrash about in a hissy. Maybe I will have to repent. Most murderers repent. Some even get paroled and return to writing. A few produce best-sellers describing how Jesus saved them from themselves and steered them onto the Road to Reformation and into the country of High Financial Cotton.

Jesus won't do for me; my muse was Greek, not Christian. She wore bed sheets, flip flops, and a cone-shaped helmet. She carried a six-foot long pencil that from a distance looked like a spear. She once mentioned Homer, calling him a stupendous bore, "always nattering on about war or naked boys throwing the discus." "He got most of his facts wrong, too," she said, "although he wasn't as inaccurate as that pipsqueak Herodotus." Several times she tore up pages I wrote, yelling, "By Heracles." But just as often she shouted "Zounds" and "Holy Cow." In some ways she wasn't a bad gal. When an acquaintance suggested I write about a town he knew named Perversion, she said, "He's a fool and a damn bad person." On my replying, saying people who loved liberty never feared license, she shouted "rubbish" and crashed my computer. She banished hard liquor from the house, and she shielded me from the Harpies that prey upon scribblers and wreck homes. "You've been a good boy too long to become bad," she said once when a lascivious thought belly-danced into my head and almost onto a page. "Forget about foxy trots and Tennessee waltzes and write down this pun. It's profound and was one of Zeus's favorites, though Hera didn't care for it. By the by Hera was a cold-hearted and unaffectionate empuse, and she cheated at dominos and Canasta. What a mistake Zeus made marrying her! Anyway here is the pun: 'Things rubbed against a grater become lesser.'" When I frowned after hearing the pun, she said, "Try this one; it's a dandy: 'Presence of mind is admirable, but when a man is freezing, he shouldn't try to keep cool.'"

Oh, gee, I guess I'll resuscitate her. She prevents me from getting lonely and keeps my mind percolating, although frequently the brew of ideas is stale. In any case an imaginary character can't be strangled, much less reduced to dog poop. And besides, my muse didn't die. On returning in January from the Caribbean cruise Vicki and I took during the Christmas holidays, I found a sheaf of papers amid the mail on the kitchen table. The pages were in her handwriting. Although I didn't see her on the promenade deck or in the dining room, she must have accompanied us because some of the sheets described bits of the trip.

Vacations are not restful. They shatter the equanimity of routine. In loosening the ties of the workaday, vacations invite, almost force, a person to mull possibilities. They cause anxiety as people ponder filling their free time. Ignoring the travel section in the Sunday paper becomes almost impossible, and friends lose individuality, flocking like starlings in the fall, whirling about and asking the same importunate question, "What are you going to do this year?" To avoid the tension fomented by possibility, I've imposed habit upon the Christmas vacation, becoming, in my muse's word, a "nautomaniac." As a person ages, he grows increasingly cautious, however. In the past I flew from Connecticut to Florida the day our cruise was scheduled to sail. This year I worried so much about being snowbound and missing the sailing that we flew to Fort Lauderdale two days before the cruise departed. "The last time I saw Fort Lauderdale

The Splendour Falls

was in 1960," I told Vicki. "I wonder what the city will be like." "Very different," Vicki said. Vicki was right.

The city had changed, but my thoughts were flanged, locking me into habitual observation. I roamed the beach noticing birds, not people, royal terns, sanderlings trusting as kittens, and black skimmers that would have appeared sinister had they not been so beautiful with dark caps and blade-like orange bills dripping black at the tips. A corroboree of yellow chevroned parakeets jangled amid the palms growing beside Sea Breeze Boulevard. Fan-tailed grackles swarmed sidewalks cadging crumbs, and near the Sawgrass Recreation Park at the edge of the Everglades, ospreys hovered then dove for fish while a morticians' convention of black vultures hunched in dead trees. Vicki and I spent a day riding the water taxi. Spiky iguanas sunned atop breakwaters, and a manatee floated just below the surface of the New River, looking like a plastic clothes bag, spread out and slightly sooty. The palatial houses and yachts moored along the waterway were comedic in their extravagance. "No matter how high man climbs," Vicki said, "he can't hide his tail." "Yes," I said, "and the one communist that capitalism will never vanquish is cancer—the ultimate social leveler."

Near Sunrise Boulevard Vicki and I got off the taxi and walked to the Galleria Mall. The mall resembled an aquarium with crowds schooling through shops, many people guppies but others fighting fish. In Neiman Marcus shanks of bottled blond hair swung off shoulders of countless customers waving like fish tails. None of the customers appeared to be Christian Scientists, for most appeared to have been filleted and deboned in hopes of looking like fingerlings of angel fish, at least from a distance. A woman tried on a pair of high-heeled shoes, the toes and sides of which were spotted like the skin of a leopard. The shoes cost $1,200. "Not footwear a female worried about feeding cubs would consider buying," Vicki said. "A pittance," I said, picking up a pair of pink "Bollywood," "Christian Louboutin" platform shoes glittering like a drawer of costume jewelry, the price tag $2,725. At four o'clock at Coffee Sensations one could purchase a small coffee and a piece of "Dessert Cake" for $3.95. "I can't hang around until four," I told the clerk behind the counter. "How about giving me the daylight savings price?" "What?" the clerk said. "Daylight savings turns three into four," I explained. "No, you have to wait until four," the clerk answered. "What did you expect?" Vicki said. "Play of mind," I said. Before we left the mall, however, Vicki and I picked out the cakes we would have eaten at four. While I selected a slice of turtle cheese cake, Vicki chose a piece of coconut cake. "Damn good," she said to the clerk, picking a napkin off the counter and wiping her lips as we left the café.

During the school year I rarely meet anyone other than students and teachers. In part cruises are alluring because they vary one's acquaintances. A British commando taught physical education to armed forces in half a dozen countries. "I always carried a walnut in my pocket when I lectured on the prostate," he said. "After I retired and became an usher at Westminster, I still carried the walnut for good luck." A man from Kidderminster traveled the world selling carpets. A Frenchman flew Mirage airplanes for twenty years. A woman owned trailer parks. A salesman said he liked to sleep on airplanes. When the person sitting beside him insisted on talking, the salesman stated that he worked for the Internal Revenue Service. "That usually shut folks up. Once or twice people changed seats." The first night on the cruise a couple eating dinner close to us had to wait fifteen minutes before being seated. "I want you to do something to make me feel good," the man said to the head waiter. When the head waiter looked puzzled, the man repeated, "I want you to make me feel good," adding, "A glass of merlot would make me feel good." The man's insistent wheedling made me squirm.

During another dinner I heard someone ask four times, "What did he do during the Civil War?" After the last repetition, I wanted to say, "Damn it to hell. Ask the son of a bitch. He's always nattering on about Perryville and Signal Mountain, blue coats and grey coats, Andersonville and Camp Morton. Of course he is a monumental liar, and I doubt he ever left his mama's parlor." A woman from another cruise ship stepped in front of me on the pier in Nassau. Tattooed on the back of the woman's calves were Disney characters, on the left calf Sylvester the Cat, on the right Donald Duck dressed as a dominatrix, in his hands a sheaf of different sized whips, one size, I suppose, not fitting or spanking all bottoms. "Where do you suppose Tweety Bird is nesting?" Vicki said. "Oh, Lord," I exclaimed. Still, the "corker" was something a guide at the Soufriere Volcano on St. Lucia said. "A poisonous snake cannot kill a mongoose because the mongoose has only one vein in its entire body. And this vein," the guide declared, "is found in the mongoose's tail." "That is amazing, almost unbelievable," a woman said to me after listening to the guide. "Absolutely amazing," I replied then walked away to look at a pool belching boiling water. During the second half of the cruise several hundred jazz enthusiasts boarded the boat, and I spent hours listening to ragtime and tunes from Tin Pan Alley: "Dance of the Grizzly Bear," "Candlestick Rag," and "A Chicken Ain't Nothing But a Bird." "Way down on Bimini Bay" absinthe made the heart grow fonder. "Don't Bring Lulu," Johnny advised; she is as "wild as any Zulu." I've "been a good old wagon," I thought one day after a musical afternoon, but I've "done broken down." Five cruise ships docked the same day on St. Maarten, spewing ten thousand passengers into Philipsburg. Late that afternoon when the passengers returned to the ships, the dock was as crowded as the Atlanta airport on Friday evening. "Somewhere in town there must be a sign that reads, 'White People, Don't Let the Sun

Set on You Here,'" a man standing next to me said, watching people streaming into their boats.

Women swim topless at Shell Beach on St. Bart's. I couldn't tell, however, whether middle-aged sunbathers were male or female, especially, to use Vicki's phrase, if they were "overcome by girth." When I tried to describe the bathers, I could not pull the word *odalisque* from memory. "Words are slipping from me," I said to Vicki. "Who cares?" Vicki said. "Just go with the ebb." For her part Vicki is a close observer. "That man over there," she said pointing to a man standing beside his wife on Brimstone Hill on St. Kitts, "is too solicitous and well-behaved to be a good husband. Good husbands are grumpy and unpleasant like you. Any woman who looks at you and sees you frowning can tell immediately that you're a good husband." Being dubbed an adequate spouse did not ameliorate the worry of losing words. I tried to compensate by noting names, shops on Antigua, for example, "Fat Boy, Smart Boy Restaurant," "Thriller Sports Bar," "Spring Bling Car Wash," and "Sam and Dave's Laundry."

I did nothing systematically on the cruise. One evening I sat near the stern of the boat and ate key lime pie and watched lights flicker like sparklers along the Cuban coast. Above the land, clouds gathered in great purple anvils. For a moment the moon glowed like a pearl, but then hammers pounded the anvils forging rain. In harbors I ignored cruise ships and looked at the small inter-island freighters. Almost all were battered and seemed lifted from the browning pages of crazed books, in St. Vincent, *Belle*, for example, her superstructure white, the hull blue but dented and wearing rusty near the water line, a single black crane scratchy above the holds; and the *Persia II*, smaller, the superstructure white again, but the hull blue, brown, and green, her crane a claw, nearby in front of the wheelhouse a white cylindrical fuel tank. The coasters were salt-worn and listed like old men slumping off their pelvises. Reading colors vision, however, and even though I saw freighters clearly, I imagined musky winds, the pied wantonness of yellowish sands, and a small harbor, lianas dripping over the channel like perspiration, amid them a rickety dock at the end of which a warehouse slumped stupefied and hot. Beside a corner of the warehouse a single golden trumpet tree bloomed, the fists of yellow flowers too heavy for the tree's tired limbs, causing them to sag at the elbow. Beyond the warehouse a scarred dirt road ran out of sight collapsing amid heat bucketing heavy off the leaves of a breadfruit tree.

Perhaps in reaction to the politicians in the United States, all of whom seem blighted saplings and who once they achieve influence spread the spores of cultural and moral dieback, I was attracted by healthy trees, initially those that turned bits of the landscape into impressionistic paintings: bauhinia purple and pink with "orchids," tulip trees, their branches candelabras of scarlet chalices, and yellow bells although this last was frequently grown as a hedge. Often planted nearby were jungle flame and assorted gingers: sea shell ginger, ginger lilies, and cock of the walk red ginger. The blossoms attracted hummingbirds, on Dominca, the purple throated carib, and on St. Lucia, the Antillean crested. On cannonball trees gloves of pink and orange flowers bloomed amid tangled sleeves of stems. The pods on tamarind looked like fat gnomes. While the seed pods of Poinciana were black and curved like the eyebrows of mythological giants, slabs of sea grape were vibrant, radiating color, the cuts orange and red, looking like the sun's last burst before it slipped into shadows and settled into night. From baobabs seeds dangled in stuffed purses tied to the ends of narrow belts. On almond purses were smaller, only big enough to hold a handful of change.

While fruits on pandanus resembled pineapples, those on cocoa looked like small deflated footballs. Inside the balls a sticky white pulp surrounded the seeds. I chewed several; they tasted sweet and fruity. I sampled several fruits, always picking them off the ground and not biting into them unless they had begun to rot. In the botanical garden in St. Vincent, I bit into an apple-sized fruit fallen from a tree that probably belonged in the persimmon family. A guide said the fruit was bitter and would make my tongue curl. The fruit's orange skin had turned brown and mushy, and the meat was both sour and sweet, and very good. The greenish-white fruit of the noni, a variety of mulberry, looked like a small potato. Orange eyes speckled the surface, and the fruit smelled like limburger cheese, but it tasted sugary and quenched my thirst. I did not taste any guava fruits, but on the dock at St. Maarten, I drank a "guavaberry" rum smoothie. It was purple and medicinal, restoring kick into legs worn out by climbing about the fortress above Marigot. Green and brown, and sometimes blue-tinged, geckos skittered about my every step, and when I paused, the cooing of Zenaida doves waffled through the air in soft breezes. I spent more time looking at trees than I did walking the promenade deck on the boat. Occasionally I leaned over the rail and watched brown boobies shear upward into spirals then slide down pursing flying fish, but banyans bearded with prop roots and the great seraglio fans crowning traveler's trees appealed to me more. I pulled slivers of bark from cinnamon trees and imagined myself an Arab trader traveling to Alexandria, and I turned the trunks of West Indian Mahogany into wine chests, sideboards, and highboys.

My life on the boat was cupboardy as befits a good husband and someone murderous enough to consider butchering a muse. However I did enjoy an enhancing experience that made me a true tourist and cruiser. A norovirus raged through the ship, and me. For thirty-six hours my DWV system stopped functioning, its traps exploding upwards, the cleanouts becoming straight pipes. I lost so much liquid that my legs cramped. Vicki rallied, however, and poured creeks of water down my throat. At the end of the cruise a fellow passenger who'd also had everything leached out of him except words turned to me on the dock and said, "I wish I'd scheduled my colonoscopy for this afternoon here in Fort Lauderdale rather than a week from now when I am back in Minneapolis."

Painted on a billboard in front of a hospital on St. Kitts was "Thank You for My Healing." Amen, and I never want to experience a norovirus again. In any case I, too, am home now. Yesterday Vicki and I walked the trail below Horsebarn Hill. The temperature was eight degrees, and ice had begun to wrap snags in the Fenton River. "Full parkatation weather," Vicki said, turning herself into an ambulatory hot water heater, wrapping her pipes and valves in an undershirt, a long sleeved shirt, two sweat shirts, one medium-sized, the other small, and finally the covering of the tank, a parka insulated with down. For my part I carried a notebook but didn't remove it from my coat pocket. Neither my pen nor hands worked in the cold, and besides my muse is really gone. She has decamped, leaving Connecticut for a warmer climate, "a land where avocados and bougainvillea grow," she said in a note I found on my bedside table. "I'm going to swim with white-cheeked pintails on St. Thomas and swill Banks beer on Barbados. I'm going topless, and bottomless, on St. Barts and eat chocolate croissants and drink cappuccinos at the Little Dove Bakery. I am gone for good. I am off to meet the 'Big Butter and Egg Man.' Together we'll kayak across the sunrise and zip line into the sunset. Never again will I jerk you out of bed in the middle of the night, prop your eyes open with toothpicks, and force you to write. Before I left, I removed all the thumbscrews and papers, pincers and pens from your study and carried them to the dump." "Sis boom bah!" I exclaimed when I read the note, leaping into the air like a high school cheerleader. "The print run has been good, but, Hallelujah, the scribbling is over." "The morning may be cold," I thought, looking out the bedroom window, "but the sun is shining. In a month or two the earth will stretch. Bloodroot will bloom in the side yard. The woods will shed their rust, and meadows will smell green and winy. Oh, happy, happy simple days!"